THE RELATE EXPERIENCE

Experiences of Relate Counselling

Broken, shattered and fragmented,
We stood on the edge.
A hand reached out and led us to safety.
Each week we came a little less broken;
You showed us the way back to being whole again.
We're stronger and wiser now,
All because of your gentle guidance,
Observation and skilled knowledge.
Our gratitude to you is boundless.

Tribute from a couple to their
Relate counsellor, February 2015

RB
Rossendale Books

*All profits from this book will go to Relate,
the leading national charity specialising in
relationship counselling*

Dedication

As well as its paid staff, Relate is also reliant on its wonderful volunteers who give many unpaid hours to support the work of the charity. Betty Gittins, who worked in Relate charity shops for more than 20 years and finally retired at the age of 91, is a wonderful example and this book is dedicated to Betty's memory on behalf of all our volunteers.

Published by Lulu Enterprises Inc.
3101 Hillsborough Street
Suite 210
Raleigh, NC 27607-5436
United States of America

Published in paperback 2015
Category: Reference
Copyright Alan Cooper © 2015

ISBN: 978-1-326-39293-2

Confidentiality and Reality
Author's note

There are various kinds of stories in this book. Some are actual accounts told to me and from which I have created real life stories. However, since counselling by its nature is a very private activity and confidentiality so important, client and counsellor names have been changed throughout and so have some of the details. Because of this any identification of individuals will only be speculation. Other stories are fictionalised accounts merged from similar counselling problems as told to me by counsellors and also from my own experience as a Relate counsellor for eight years. There is also a longer story about a couple which runs in episodes through the book. This is entirely fictional. Everything in the book however reflects how sessions develop within Relate counselling.

Counsellors are careful not to engage with clients in the outside world. The counselling relationship needs to be very much an experience of the counselling room in the here and now. Interaction with clients after the work is finished rarely happens. Occasionally however, there are accidental meetings, which can be amusing or sometimes poignant. A few have been told to me during the process of writing this book. I've called these 'afterwords' and have included them to give another perspective of the Relate experience.

The personal accounts from counsellors and volunteers are all actual stories either told to me or written by the individuals themselves, or in two cases, a relative.

Everything in the book is geared to the core purpose of revealing the various problems Relate helps, and what actually happens in the counselling room. In addition I have hoped to present some moving experiences in a readable and sometimes humorous way, so that reading the book is enjoyable as well as informative.

Producing this book has not cost Relate anything. **All** profits will go to support the work of Relate Shropshire, Herefordshire and North Staffordshire and to building a bursary to support clients with limited financial means.

Foreword from Chris Sherwood
Chief Executive, Relate

Relate has come a long way since it started life as the National Marriage Guidance Council in 1938 providing support to married couples going through tough times. Now in 2015, we offer a full range of services to single, cohabiting and married people including relationship counselling, sex therapy, family counselling and mediation whether it's face to face on the phone or via our online service.

Our 1,700 counsellors across our 59 centres in the UK will know of thousands of inspiring stories about people who have improved their relationships with family, friends and partners after coming to Relate. Due to their often very personal nature, these stories are rarely heard. We understand this, but it's also true that if more people spoke out about their experience of counselling, it would encourage others to seek help for relationship difficulties and improve the quality of their own lives.

It is for this reason that it is so wonderful that Alan, an accomplished writer and Chair of Relate Shropshire, Herefordshire and North Staffordshire has taken the time to put together this book, bringing a selection of these moving stories to life as told to him by counsellors and former clients across several midland counties. He is a trained Relate counsellor himself and this really comes through in the book. I believe it demonstrates the true breadth of what Relate does in a lively and accessible way.

Relationships are the glue that binds our society together and this collection of experiences demonstrates why it is so worthwhile investing in them.

Acknowledgements

This book would not have been possible without the clients, counsellors, shop staff and volunteers who have contributed stories and experiences of the work of Relate. I am also grateful to Sue Frankfort Chief Executive for Relate Shropshire, Herefordshire and North Staffordshire, whose idea this book was initially. Sue and Liz Todd, Senior Supervisor, both read the first draft of the book and offered me their advice and encouragement. Sandie Dent, administration and contracts manager, created the cover design and has also contributed to the book. Vincent Walsh of Rossendale Book has been an efficient and supportive friend to Relate in publishing *The Relate Experience*. He has been patient with my demands and also made a generous donation to the charity.

Foreword from Sue Frankfort
CEO Relate Shropshire, Herefordshire and North Staffordshire

Relate across England and Wales is a federated organisation. Our local Relate is a large family of counsellors and retail staff, supported by an admin team, all working together towards the same aim – to help people make their relationships work better. We believe this is the key to successful communities and society. Through our counselling and our ten Relate charity shops we are privileged to be involved with people's lives when they set up home, when they start a family, when families split up and when people die.

I was delighted when Alan agreed to be our chair of trustees because of his background in education and more recently as a Relate counsellor. In his retirement Alan has also become a published writer. After reading his book 'Staying Alive', which raises awareness of kidney disease by telling real life stories from people who live with it, I realised that we needed a similar way of revealing what counselling is and how our Relate works. As a result, I asked Alan to produce a book about us. He has spoken to many of our Relate family and created this readable book which truly demonstrates how an encounter with a Relate counsellor really can change lives for the better. I hope the book will encourage those who read it to spread the word, and if necessary, to pick up the phone, dial 01743 344010 and start a journey to a better life.

Love and marriage through the ages

All days are nights till I see thee
And nights bright days when dreams do show thee me.
William Shakespeare (1564 – 1616)

If our two loves be one . . . none can die.
John Donne (1571-1631)

Marriage has many pains, and celibacy has no pleasures
                              but
A second marriage is the triumph of hope over experience
 Samuel Johnson (1709-84)

With love you raise me above myself,
My good spirit, my better self
Friedrich Rückert (1788-1866)

How do I love thee? Let me count the ways.
Elizabeth Barrett Browning (1806-1861)

We must love one another or die
W.H.Auden (1907-74)

Contents

VIEWS FROM THE CLIENTS' CHAIRS

SANDRA'S JOURNEY TO RELATE

Looking back on it now, it's pretty clear to both of us that our marriage had been drifting for years. Neither of us really wanted to admit it. Harry wrapped himself up in his work, and I looked after the house and the children as well as doing my part time work as a receptionist at the local GP surgery. I suppose I was happy after a fashion, but there was this deep feeling of dissatisfaction.

'We're happy enough,' is what I used to say to friends if ever the subject of marriage came up. One of my friends went through a divorce; separated after sixteen years together. I couldn't understand why she did that. The children were still quite young. I asked her whether either of them had found someone else. 'No', she said, 'it wasn't working anymore. We just agreed it would be better for both of us'. I felt like saying 'what about the children', but I didn't. I just thought to myself that we could never do that. We were happy enough, I told myself. The truth was that we weren't.

It's hard to say what wasn't right. There are obvious things. We didn't talk much to each other. We didn't row; just went our own ways. If I was worried about anything, Harry wasn't the person I'd want to talk to. Inevitably the sex, so good when we first met and through the early years, got less frequent and quite mechanical. But we didn't talk about that either. I know now that we'd just lost the intimacy, but at the time I couldn't have said that because I wasn't actually conscious of it.

I always knew that deep down, really deep down, I still loved him. I couldn't have told you what that meant mind, but it felt like a basic fact of life. I believed we could be happier. A kind of act of faith I just hung onto. Not rational at all, but the most important things in life aren't rational.

Then several things happened more or less together. Our son William, went off to university. I'm sure I missed him more than he missed me. He didn't come home much, and when he did he wanted to meet up with his friends. Suzanne our 15 year old daughter got her first serious boyfriend and when she was at home all she seemed to want to do was phone him, text him or PM him on Facebook. My world at home became very lonely. Then Harry had a stroke. TIA the doctors called it, a kind of mini-stroke. It didn't leave any permanent damage but it felt like a warning sign to both of us. And I knew then how much I really cared about him.

It was just at that time that Tina, one of the other receptionists at the surgery, happened to mention she was going to Relate. I had no idea what that was. 'You know', she said, 'sorting out relationships and things.' I suppose I must have looked blank. 'Used to be called Marriage Guidance, but they do a lot more than that now.' I kept quiet. She didn't seem embarrassed by the idea of talking about her marriage with an organisation, but I was sure it wasn't what I wanted to do. I still told myself we were happy enough. Things would turn out OK.

But that evening Harry got home late. He sat down in front of the television and fell asleep. Suzanne was out with the boyfriend and I just felt like I didn't want to live like that for the rest of my life. Could we really go and talk about what was wrong between us? I doubted if Harry would ever agree to that. For whatever reason, when I'd made him a cup of tea, I just casually mentioned it.
"What's that?" he said.

"Tina, one of the receptionists was talking about it today."
He just grunted and slurped his tea. Suddenly it came over me. This was the man I married, the man I'd loved, and all he could do was grunt at something I said.
"Don't you want to know any more?" I said.
"What?"
"About what I just said."
"What's that?"
"Don't keep saying what!"
"What? What's got into you?"
"I said Tina and her husband were going to Relate . . . and don't say what's that!"
He tried to look interested after that, but I knew he wasn't really bothered. Strangely, that made me even more determined to tell him.

I told him the little bit I'd picked up from Tina. Then for some reason I said it.
"I was wondering if we ought to go . . ."
"Go?"
"See a counsellor . . ."
"What for?"
I don't quite know why, but I really lost it then. I think it was the way he kept saying 'what'. I just shouted and shouted. I don't know the words I said, but all the frustration inside of me poured out. Harry just looked at me without really saying anything until I finished. Then I couldn't stop crying. He can't cope with that and just went out of the room.

I don't think I've ever felt so lonely in my life as I did then, just sobbing loudly to myself. Afterwards, all I could do was go up to bed. I went fast asleep quite quickly, but woke again in the middle of the night. Harry wasn't there. I put my dressing gown on and went to find him. He was still in the living room with the television on. When he looked up at me I could see he was as unhappy as I was. Strangely, it wasn't something I'd thought about before. I sat down on the sofa next to him, but it felt as if there was an invisible gap between us. It was then I knew we needed help. After a while we went back to bed. I checked on Suzanne. It was a relief to see she was asleep in bed. She looked very peaceful and I wished I could be like her.

The next time I went into the surgery, I asked Tina a bit more about Relate. I didn't say why, but I think she guessed. She asked if I was alright. When I said everything was fine she looked at me like she didn't believe it. Later that morning she slipped me a piece of notepaper. On it was their telephone number. She didn't even look at me. It was very low key. But then we're trained in the surgery to be very confidential. And she'd written that on the piece of paper.

I rang up and got an appointment for the following week. I did say I hadn't yet persuaded Harry, but their receptionist said I could come on my own if I wanted to. Harry refused when I first told him about it. I didn't argue with him straightaway, but the following day I mentioned it again and he wanted to know more.
"They're very confidential," I said.
"How do you know?"
"It's how they have to work. Like at the doctors," I said.
I didn't know that for certain, but I was suddenly so desperate we needed help I was going to trust them whatever. He just did one of his grunts, but when I raised it a third time he said he'd go for just one session. I'd already made up my mind that there would only be one session if I didn't like it anyway.

So we went. And again. We ended up going 10 times! But I'm not sorry. With the help of Carole, our wonderful counsellor we talked about everything important in our relationship. The first session wasn't as difficult as I expected. Carole somehow managed to start us talking about the really important things without it being embarrassing. Afterwards, when I thought back on it, I was really surprised that we'd said so much. Even Harry said much more than I expected he would. During the sessions that followed, somehow we learnt more about each other and our relationship than I think we'd ever realised was possible.

I understand now why they're called Relate. That's exactly what we learnt to do. We had to do homework. If that sounds odd, it's not like school homework. We had to learn to spend time on our relationship like we had in those early years. When I thought about it, that's what happens completely naturally when you are young. Like Suzanne and her boyfriend. We relearnt consciously how to relate with each other. And now a year later, our marriage is as good as it ever was. Or maybe it's better. We know each other a lot better too. Tina noticed. 'Alright was it?' she said after a few weeks. I just grinned. She knew. And I could see the difference in her.

Even Suzanne noticed.
"You two . . ." she said one evening after about the seventh session, "you're like . . . different."
There was a grin on her face when she said it.
"Oh, so you do notice we're around occasionally," I said.
"What?"
"Don't say that Suzanne, I don't like it."
The grin became a cross pout.
"I'm sorry, it's just . . ."
I didn't finish. She'd already turned away to look at a text on her iPhone. Whatever it was seemed to improve her mood again. I managed to resist the temptation to ask about it.
"You were saying we were different?"
"You and dad. Less naggy, yeah. 'Cept then . . ."
The grin was back.
"I know. I'm sorry."
"Cool."
And with that she was off to her bedroom.

I found myself laughing. A few weeks earlier I don't think I could have done that. You only get so many chances in life. Carole gave us the opportunity to build our lives again. Another chance in fact. I'm really glad we took it.

HOW ISABEL'S LIFE WAS TRANSFORMED

Can you counsel a six year old? It was her grandad who first suggested it. He's had counselling himself and thought it might help. As granny I was doubtful, but I could see little Isabel was really struggling. And there were a lot of reasons why. A year earlier, her dad left. The relationship between mum and dad had not been good, but the split was still a problem for her. Shortly before that, her cat was killed in a road accident. Her mum was not in a particularly good place, and as the sensitive girl she is, that was certainly transferring itself to her.

But Isabel had another problem too. Her nine year old sister Karen is autistic. At her best, she's humorous and loving. At her most difficult, she demands attention and has melt-downs if she doesn't get what she immediately wants. That means she loses control, shouts, screams and cries completely irrationally. Change, as with most of those on the autistic spectrum, causes all sorts of anxieties. Karen finds it hard to start eating, has particular problems with going to the toilet, and will refuse to do even the things she really wants to do. The default position is 'No!' 'I am not going to see Cinderella!' was a recent statement, yet when she got to the cinema she loved it.

So it's hardly surprising Isabel picked up some of Karen's behaviour. Transitions for her were identified as problems, going to school, going to see dad, staying with anyone else invoked what seemed like separation anxiety mixed in with worries whether mum was going to be alright. She easily got tearful and scared of new things. At home, something of a role reversal operated; she was the one who often had to give in. Not doing so could easily lead to major problems with Karen.

So grandad and I suggested some counselling support. We knew Relate worked in schools, but didn't know if it was possible to work with anyone as young as six. Isabel's mum decided to explore it, and a very thoughtful receptionist put her in touch with Jean, who had skills with young children.

As granny, although I knew I had a special relationship with Isabel, I felt at one remove. Over the next few weeks we looked for signs of progress. And the confidentiality of the counselling relationship meant that even mum didn't know too much about what was happening during the half hour sessions inside the counselling room.

What we did know was that Isabel was changing. We could see it in her behaviour. The anxieties didn't disappear overnight, but they certainly seemed less intense. When mum left her and Karen with us, the tears when mum drove off became a thing of the past. She was happy to be with us, explore the garden, start learning the names of flowers and throw food pellets into the fish pond. She was beginning to seem altogether more settled. We could see the anxieties going from our daughter too, and of course, in turn this helped Isabel to be less anxious.

On one occasion, mum wasn't able to take Isabel to her session with Jean, and I took her instead. I could see how happily she went into the counselling room with smiles of obvious pleasure. For me, it felt strange to be sitting in the quiet waiting room just outside. Then, towards the end of the half hour there were noises, distinct sounds of Isabel roaring like a lion, a little game she loved to play with grandad and me when she stayed. There were other strange sounds too, like Jean perhaps responding. I knew one of the things Jean did with her was to use toy animals in little game situations. That's something Isabel had let slip about her sessions. The noises went on for some time. I sat intrigued. It would have been great to have gone in and watched, but of course I knew I couldn't do that.

After some while, definitely more than half an hour, the door flew open and a radiant Isabel came bouncing out, full of smiles and obvious energy. She was followed by a red faced Jean, looking perhaps a bit guilty. I wondered what she would be thinking, but I didn't ask. A friendly grin seemed sufficient. Jean grinned back. It felt like unspoken communication.

In my car on the way home, Isabel chattered and chattered. It was happy talk, like something very special had happened. I'm sure now it was a turning point. I've speculated that all the animal noises were an intentional release of tension after perhaps some very important counselling work. There's no doubt it proved a crucial moment in Isabel's development. Since then, she's had so much more confidence, and all the separation anxiety seems dissipated.

Counselling sessions carried on for a while after this. Consolidation of what was learned we assumed. Change needs to be embedded for it to be permanent. But Isabel's been so different since then. Her teacher says she's been more confident at school, and certainly at home she's more relaxed, more settled altogether. Another cat had to be put down recently. She coped well with that, grieved briefly and got over it. Aged seven now, she's a new girl.

I feel privileged to have taken Isabel to that vital session and to have seen her bounding out of the counselling room. I've thought about it since, tried to make a kind of sense of it in my own head. The best image I can come up with is that it was like a huge weight had lifted from her. Counselling can be incredibly powerful, and a great force for good.

GETTING STARTED

The first session

"We've been married three years, known each other five. Everything was great. I've never loved anyone as much as Dave. He was the answer to all my dreams."

I'm sitting next to Jo, listening to her saying this. I can't believe we're here in this room, talking to a counsellor, a woman called Stevie. When we arranged it, I thought it would be a bloke, but it's actually Stephanie. She seems pleasant enough. The eyes are brown and kind, that's how I judge people, even though she's not smiling. Her hands are in front of her, in her lap, over a kind of spotted dress. She's got grey hair, about fifty I guess.

"We knew we both wanted children. Not long after we got married, I stopped . . ."

Jo's suddenly gone shy and I can't help smiling.

"You know . . ."

"The contraceptive pill," Stevie says.

It sounds so matter-of-fact when she says that. Like it's alright to say things. Jo starts talking again.

"Last year, little Ruby was born. It was like a dream come true."

And suddenly I can see Jo is crying. There's a box of tissues on a table beside where I'm sitting. I nudge her and pass one over. She takes it.

"Sorry," she says, when she's wiped her eyes, "I don't know why I'm crying."

Stevie just smiles very faintly. "A dream come true," she says, looking at me, like it's my turn to say something.

"Yeah, we both love her," I say.

"So, do you want to say why you're here?"

I look at Jo, and she looks at me. There's a smudge on her face where the make-up's run a bit. I don't say anything about that. I can see Jo wants me to explain.

"It's just . . . well you've changed since Ruby was born," I say to Jo, "Like I'm a nuisance now, not your husband."

"That's not fair!" Jo says straightaway. "You just don't understand!"

There's a pause. I don't know what to say.

"What doesn't he understand," Stevie says.

"About how it is, when you've got a baby. She's with my mum now, but I'm still thinking about her, wondering if she's alright."

"You know she will be," I say.

"Doesn't stop me thinking about her."

"Do you want to explain a bit more, Jo?" Stevie says.

"It's nature. You're just wrapped up in it all. Ruby has to come first, but it's so tiring. There's washing and cleaning and nappies and all that, and I'm up most nights, or I'm listening out for her. I just get so tired . . ."

"And what about me?" I say.

"Exactly! You think about your needs, not mine and Ruby's."

"How can you say that?"

"Well it's true . . ."

"I know Ruby comes first, but she doesn't have to take up all the time!"

"That's not fair, Dave, and you know it isn't . . ."

I can feel myself getting angry. It's like we're heading for one of our rows. Stevie is looking across at me now, like she knows something, but she stays quiet. Seeing her watching makes me stop, and there's an awkward silence. Jo looks like she might start crying again, and I'm feeling guilty.

"Is this what often happens?" Stevie says.

"We never used to argue," Jo says, "You've changed Dave . . ."

"It's not me, it's you . . ."

"Perhaps it's being parents," Stevie says.

Then she asks me about what I mean when I talk about my needs. And she asks about closeness; and then sex. It shocks me at first, but I have to admit that's part of the problem. Well a big part actually. I'm a normal man after all, and she's so often too tired now . . . since Ruby was born.

"I knew I'd have to wait a few weeks after," I say, "but it's a year now, and we've not got back to normal."

"What's normal, Dave?" Stevie says.

She seems completely OK about asking a question like that. I'm amazed, but it helps, her not having a problem with it and I feel myself able to tell her.

"Well, two, maybe three times a week," I say.

"Or more . . ."

I look at Jo when she says that. There's a bit of a shy smile on her face now and I can't help smiling back because I know she's right.

"And now?" Stevie says.

"Once a week . . . if I'm lucky."

I wonder if Stevie's going to take Jo's side over this. Women sticking together and all that, but she doesn't. She just nods at me like she understands. But it's not just sex. We used to be very close. I could talk to Jo about all sorts of things, and it isn't like that now. We used to go out to gigs and clubs and things, and we hardly ever do that since Ruby. I tell Stevie all that and it feels OK. She just lets me talk. Then Jo talks about how it is for her. How she really does get very tired and how it's also about what she calls 'emotional tiredness'. She's not said that before, and I'm not really sure I know what she means.

Then we seem to have come to the end of the first session. I'm amazed. It's gone really quickly. Stevie asks how we feel now. It's an odd question I think and I just say 'fine'. She looks at me as if she doesn't really believe me. Jo answers by saying she's glad she's had

24

the chance to say how she feels without me getting angry. That's a shock, but I know it's true.

"You're like our referee," she says to Stevie.

As soon as she says that, I know it's true. I say I agree.

"And you Dave? Does it feel like you've had the chance to say how it is for you?"

"Yeah," I say, and when I say it, and that's true too. I really have.

We arrange to see Stevie again, next week. When we walk out of the offices it's still light. I realise I feel a bit drained, but not in a bad way. Jo takes hold of my hand and squeezes it. There's a pub almost next door to the Relate offices and she asks if I fancy a pint.

"I'll drive us home," she says.

Of course I agree.

"Mum won't mind a few more minutes," she says.

Sitting together, me with my pint and Jo with an orange juice feels different. Like we've got a bit closer together. Neither of us says anything for a while, but it's not one of those awkward silences we've been having.

"She's alright, isn't she," Jo says.

I have to agree. It's true. Stevie's already helped us.

"Cheers," I say, lifting my pint and smiling.

Jo lifts her orange and clinks it against my glass. A few more sessions doesn't feel like too bad an idea after all.

WHAT THE TEXT SAID

I don't think I've ever felt so bad as the day I looked in Jack's mobile phone and saw that sexy message to some woman called Michelle. Lots of things slotted into place; the extra evening appointments, the need to shower when he got in and not feeling like sex. When before in our marriage had that ever happened? I scrolled back to see if there were other texts, but that was the only one. He must have got rid of the rest, but missed this one. There was a numbness at first, like . . . this couldn't be true. Then I felt sick, as if I was actually going to vomit there and then. Next, I wanted to throw the phone as far as I could as if that would get what I'd discovered out of my life.

He'd come home drunk. Saturday evening out with some mates he said. I didn't disbelieve him. It was something he did occasionally. I didn't mind. It meant I could have a girls' night out and leave him in charge of the children without feeling guilty. He'd gone up to bed and left his phone on the table. I don't really know why I looked at it. Some sixth sense that something wasn't quite right perhaps. Whatever, I looked, and life would never be the same again.

When I went upstairs he was already asleep and snoring. I got in beside him. I felt like shaking him and demanding to know who Michelle was, but I knew he'd be too drunk to know what I was talking about. Instead I just rolled over the other way. I couldn't touch him. At some point in the night he turned towards me and I wriggled across to the edge of the bed.

That night was long. I didn't sleep much. At about seven o'clock, when it was light I got up. Jack was still asleep. Once more the urge was to shake him, but instead I put my dressing gown on, went downstairs, fed the cat and walked into the garden. It was a bright spring morning and there were blossoms on the apple trees. Normally I'd have been happy, but that morning I just felt really bad, like I'd been betrayed and there was no going back.

Not long after I turned to see Jack coming through the kitchen door towards me. He looked awful. His clothes, obviously the ones from the night before, were crumpled and creased, and his eyes were bloodshot. He hadn't combed his hair. When he got close I could still smell the alcohol on him. I just turned away, not wanting to have anything to do with him. When he put his hand on my shoulder I shrugged it off.

"Vic, what's up?"

I remember my arms were across my chest as I stayed with my back to him. I didn't answer.

"Vic . . ."

Still I didn't respond.

"What's up, Vic?"

I turned round suddenly. I was aware of him stepping back as if he was in shock.

"Michelle . . ." I said, "mean anything to you?"

His face changed, I'm sure of it.

"So it does."

"What?"

"Don't pretend Jack. The text to Michelle? 'I could lick your nipples'?"

All the anger in me was boiling up to the surface. I want to hit out at him, really hurt him. I could see his brain working out what I might know.

"I can explain . . ."

"Well, I'm waiting. . . ."

"It's not like it seems."

"Really?"

I can be very sarcastic when I want to be.

"It was just a laugh . . ."

"So why aren't I laughing?"

"Look Vic, there's nothing in it."

"So who is she?"

"Boss's PA. She's just flirty, that's all."

I look at him. I can't believe he's saying that; as if it's nothing. But then he can be very stupid. He tries to take me in his arms, but I step back. I can't have anything to do with him.

That was a terrible day. Every so often he tried to get me to soften and to talk to him, but I wouldn't. He accused me of sulking, which at the time I thought was unfair. Looking back on it now, I suppose that was right, but I just couldn't bring myself to talk to him. I was in a dark place, there seemed no way out. Towards the end of the day Jack started suggesting we went somewhere to get some help, but I couldn't believe that would make any difference. I was convinced he was having an affair. All I could see at that time was the end of our marriage.

That night I wouldn't sleep with him at all. I went into our daughter Karen's room. She was away at university. Through that night I imagined having to tell her we were splitting up. I cried myself to sleep. Once I woke up and there was an owl hooting somewhere outside. It seemed like a really bad omen. I don't think I slept very well and when I woke up I didn't know if I was going into work. Then Jack was at the bedroom door. He was up and showered and ready for work, and in his hand was a cup of tea for me. Although he looked like he'd had a bad night, he was all smart in his suit. He put the tea on the bedside table.

"I'm going to get us some help," he said.

I didn't know what he was talking about. He could see that.

"Relate. I've found them online," he said.

"What's that?"

"Counselling. They do counselling for couples. It's what we need."

"How do you know I'll go with you?"

"I don't," he said, "but I'll make an appointment and go myself if you won't come. I've got to go to work now. See you later," he said.

I didn't know what to think. It was certainly a surprise, him taking the initiative like that. I got up and looked at myself in the mirror. What I saw was terrible. My hair was a mess, my eyes were dark where I'd been crying and one of them was a bit bloodshot. I looked like a battered wife, although Jack had never been like that. I really didn't want to go to work, but I didn't want to stay at home on my own either, so I got myself sorted and went in.

When I got there, Stella, who sits next to me in the office, could see I was in a bad way.

"You alright?" she said as soon as she saw me.

"Yes, I'm fine."

I knew she didn't believe me, but she had the sense not to say anything then. It was only when we had our break she took me aside and wanted to know more. I had to tell her, even though I'd decided before I left home I wasn't going to talk about it.

"You sure he's having an affair?" Stella said.

"Well what was that text all about?"

"You know what men are like. Might be just what he says, flirty, ego trip stuff."

I wasn't sure what to make of that. Then I told Stella about him wanting to make a Relate appointment.

"Go," she said straightaway, "you need whatever it is sorted out."

"What, counselling?"

"Why not? There's a Relate counsellor lives a few door down from us. She's lovely . . ."

"Washing dirty linen in public?"

"No one else will know. I talk to this woman, Jane, her name is, and I've no idea who she's counselling."

"Really?"

I was looking at Stella then, wondering if she'd ever been.

"You and Phil, have you ever had counselling?" I said.

"No, but I would if I thought things were going wrong. Less expensive than a divorce."

That made me think. Did I really want to finish with Jack? After all, we'd been together more than twenty years. Maybe Stella was right. I knew I felt better after talking to her. Like there might be light at the end of the tunnel. I think I really decided then that if Jack made an appointment, I'd go with him.

That evening he was already home when I got in. I didn't say anything, just waited to see what he'd say. I went into the kitchen and bashed the pots around a bit getting some food ready for us. After a while he came in all tentative, like he was trying to test the mood. I think he wanted to put his arms around me, but I kept moving, making it clear I wasn't up for that. Eventually he had to say something.
"You alright?" he said.
"What do you think?"
I more or less spat it at him. He looked a bit shocked. For a while he didn't say anything more. Then he came out with it.
"I've made an appointment."
Still I ignored him for a moment. I was trying to weight up inside how I was going to respond.
"It's on Thursday evening."
"So?"
"Wondered if you wanted to come with me."
"I'll think about it."
He backed off then, went out of the kitchen while I got on with the dinner.

I stayed icy that evening and still slept in Karen's room. But I did know I'd accompany Jack to Relate. It was a better night and I didn't cry. The next morning I was up first. I wondered if he'd say anything more about the Relate appointment before he went to work, but he didn't. I was glad about that. Admitting I was going wasn't something I was quite ready to do. When I got to work, Stella wanted to know what had happened. I told her I'd probably go and she said she was pleased. Wanted to know when I was going to tell Jack.

"Do it tonight, Vic," she said, "he needs to know."

"After what he's done?"

"Don't play games," she said.

That made me angry for a while. I think I said something like 'what about him?' Stella didn't respond to that. As usual, I thought about it afterwards, and decided she was right.

That evening I told him when he asked me. I got the information and said I'd meet him there since it was an appointment after work for both of us. Part of me wanted to sleep in my own bed that night, but I still didn't feel like I could after what had happened and probably a bit of pride wouldn't let me give in that easily. I got into Karen's bed again, and decided that the next night would depend on what happened in the counselling session.

*

Jenny met us in the waiting room. She seemed very approachable and invited us into a room that felt very private. It was big enough for me to sit next to Jack without feeling too close, and Jenny sat in front of us, at a bit of an angle. I was surprised it didn't feel threatening in any way. She wanted to know some basic details from us first, and then asked us why we'd come. I looked at Jack. I was determined he was going to have to be the one to say. It was his idea to have the appointment, and after all, he was the one who'd done wrong. He looked at me before starting as if to say 'is it alright'.

I just raised my eyebrows and shrugged my shoulders. I could feel Jenny watching me do that.

He said what he'd said to me, about it being a 'harmless flirtation'. I noticed Jenny looking at me when he said that, and as soon as he'd finished she asked me if I thought it was harmless. Of course I said it wasn't and said I found it very hard to believe that was all it was. She asked me how I felt, and I explained how I was really hurt by it all. I got the impression she understood that.

31

What did surprise me was that she started asking us about our marriage and how it was after more than twenty years together. That made me think, and I had to admit that some of the closeness of the first years of our marriage had gone. Jenny didn't say all that much, but she did seem to be able to ask questions that got us to tell her about us, even things I hadn't really thought about before. I guessed that was true for Jack as well. We even talked a bit about sex, and I had to admit it wasn't as good as it once was. Jack agreed about that.

"So, Jack, when you say you had a 'harmless flirtation'," Jenny said towards the end of our first session, "are you really saying you were looking for something a bit more?"
"No . . ." he said, and stopped.
"Maybe you didn't realise it?"
"I don't know . . ." he said.
She waited. It was very quiet in the room at that point. Jenny just sat there watching us before turning her attention to me.
"And maybe, Vic," she said, "you were so hurt because you already sensed things weren't like you wanted them to be, and here was Jack, looking elsewhere, even if he didn't quite realise what he was trying to do?"
It felt right when she put it like that. I nodded, and I could see Jack nodding too, like he was getting the point.

"So perhaps what needs to happen," Jenny said "is to work with your relationship and see how you can both work together to make it more satisfying for both of you . . . if that's what you want of course."
I knew it was, and it was a relief to see Jack agreeing too. The session came to an end there, and we agreed to more sessions to do what Jenny suggested.

When we drove home, neither of us said much, but once we were indoors, Jack turned towards me with his arms out. I let him hug me. I couldn't help a few tears, and I think that was true of him too. He held me quite tightly for what felt like a long time and neither of us said anything. I don't think we needed to. The closeness was what spoke for us.

That night I returned to our bed. It didn't feel difficult. We both knew there was more to be done to get our relationship back to where it once had been. That was something we hadn't even realised before we went to see Jenny. And for the first time I think I believed Jack really had had nothing more than a flirtation. Although it wasn't harmless, it had been something that told us both things weren't right between us.

We saw Jenny for five more sessions after that first one. In the process we both learnt a lot about ourselves and about each other. We found ourselves admitting things we hadn't been able to see before. Each session was hard in some ways, a bit like bloodletting, but with Jenny there to hold us together, we could face up to things that had gone wrong between us. When we finished our last session I knew I was really glad we'd gone, and I was grateful to Jack for having the courage to ring up Relate, especially when Jenny said that men rarely did that. I know our relationship is a lot better now and I don't think he'll be tempted by Michelle or any other flirty woman in the future.

The week after we finished with Jenny, Karen came back on holiday from uni. Two days into her time at home she said to me
"What's got into you two?"
"What do you mean?" I said.
"You and dad. You're being so nice to each other. It's a bit creepy isn't it?"
"Creepy?"
"Well, you used to snap at each other. You don't do that now. I've even see you holding hands!"
She's laughing.

"You youngsters, do you think us older ones can't be in love too?"

"In love?" she said, "I've never heard you say that before."

It was a bit of a shock really. I was amazed at what she said, that she'd been aware of how we'd been with each other. And at that moment I decided I'd tell her we'd been to Relate. She was a bit shocked at first, but said she was glad. And that was it. She went upstairs to get herself ready for an evening out with her friends.

I told Jack. He was amused, but like me, pleased that she'd noticed the difference. It felt like a validation of how our relationship had improved. Once she'd gone out, we opened a bottle of wine and drank to our new relationship. And it really did feel like we'd made a new start. To anyone who found themselves as a crisis point like us, I'd certainly say what Stella said to me. Go to Relate and get help to sort it out.

BEING GOOD ENOUGH

"I felt like Cinderella. Like my place was in the kitchen, a servant, while everyone else enjoyed the food and wine of the celebration. I knew it was Karl's occasion, inviting his former university friends to share a meal with the family, his new family. That wasn't a problem, and I didn't object when he wanted to hold the event at his mother's house over in Norwich, the closest central point to where his friends lived. But I didn't bargain for everything that happened that evening.

His mother is German, from a town somewhere in Bavaria. Small town German, and everything that goes with that. Her son was positioned at the head of the table, and in my place next to him . . . there was Sarah, his eight year old daughter, while I was expected to be the kitchen maid. I could feel the anger rising in me through the evening. Karl was chatting, being his usual expansive self, oblivious of all the under currents around him, while I was fuming. It all felt so wrong, and so unfair. Don't get me wrong. I love Karl, always have done, but that doesn't prevent me getting very angry with him."

Saying what happened again after a few years have passed brings it all back for Joanna. Karl takes up the story. "I suppose when two families unite there are bound to be problems. We had this vision of everyone liking each other and enjoying the benefits of new brothers and sisters. A perfect family in fact. But it didn't work out like that. Thinking back on it, we trying too hard, and the tensions kept rising. It wasn't helped by the way other people reacted. My Catholic background didn't help. Separation and divorce were really frowned on and there were remarks and innuendos. Maybe we were very sensitive to it, not helped by our own feelings of guilt, but it was definitely hurtful. Both of us, inside ourselves, knew our previous marriages weren't working, and we were doing the right thing. But we needed help, and that's where Relate came in."

"I was the one who first made contact," says Joanna. "I just knew we couldn't go on like that. When I rang up, I said I wasn't sure if Karl would be prepared to come along. It was a relief to know I could go myself. But when I told Karl, he was happy to come with me. He knew we had a problem we had to sort. We met Rebecca, the counsellor. Immediately we warmed to her. It wasn't difficult to tell her about our stories."

"She wasn't judgemental at all," says Karl, "and that was such a relief after what we'd experienced. Gradually we were able to present a picture of how complicated our lives had become. My mother had especially annoyed us by sending us a Bavarian *au pair* to teach Joanna the 'right way' to run the family. She lasted two weeks. Ending that arrangement wasn't easy. Mother couldn't accept that her way wasn't necessarily 'right'. One of the most important things we learned from Rebecca was that everyone had a different perspective. Even Joanna and I, although we shared the same needs and desires, didn't always have exactly the same view or opinion. That felt important, and liberating. But it always felt like Rebecca was on our side, helping us to find the right way forward for us."

"We both had families from our previous partners," Joanna says. "Karl had more children than I did, and that was an issue for me. In particular, Sarah, his eldest daughter felt like a problem. I tried very hard to get on with her. I suggested we did things together, girly things like having our nails done, but I felt she rejected my attempts to be a friendly mother figure. That hurt. Rebecca helped me to see I was trying too hard, wanting to get it right. She suggested that Sarah was likely to see me as usurping her place with her father. With Rebecca's help, I developed a more laid back approach, and gradually our relationship improved."

"I think it was easier for me because Joanna hasn't got a son," Karl says. "That kind of usurping role of taking over the mother, leading to what Freud called the Oedipus complex, wasn't a problem for me. And anyway, like most men I think, I tend to be less conscious of the emotional side of things. I wasn't fully aware of how difficult the relationship between Sarah and Joanna had become. It took Rebecca to help me to see that."

"Our regular counselling sessions lasted quite some time, and things improved greatly," Joanna says, "so that we felt we could stop going. We moved house, just a few miles, to make a fresh start away from critical eyes. And we got married, even inviting Rebecca to come along. She felt she couldn't, as it wasn't appropriate given her role as counsellor, and we accepted that. But we knew she had played a very important part in helping us to consolidate our relationship to the point at which we could marry. For quite some time after the wedding things went very well. Until the celebration for Karl's university friends . . ."

"If ever there was a real crisis in our relationship, that was it," says Karl. "Without thinking about it, I accepted mother's offer to hold the celebration for my East Anglian based university friends in her large house in Norwich. Unfortunately, the occasion opened up old wounds with a vengeance. Joanna has already explained how she felt like Cinderella. It was mother's idea to put Sarah next to me, and I suspect for Sarah, out of awareness, there was some satisfaction in that . . . and maybe for me too, wanting to include Sarah out of a feeling of guilt. I was blissfully unaware of any problem, simply enjoying a convivial evening with old friends. All the children were there too, and I thought it would help cement our blended family. How wrong I was!"

"Late into the evening when the last guest had gone," says Joanna, "we went to bed. I wasn't in the mood for talking, so I didn't say how I felt. Karl, happily tipsy, didn't notice anything wrong and went straight off to sleep. I lay there unable to get rid of all the emotions inside me and unable to settle. In the end, in the depth of the night, I got up, got dressed, woke and dressed my two girls and set off in the car back to the midlands. It could easily have been the end of our relationship."

"And when I woke up the following morning," Karl says, "it was to discover Joanna was gone, taking our car with her. All I could do was gather up my children together with as much of the luggage as I could manage and catch the train into London and back out again to get home. This time Joanna wasn't the only angry person. It really was a make or break moment. The only thing we thought we could do to save our relationship was to go back to Relate and begin another set of counselling sessions with Rebecca."

"Because she knows us and our story so well it was possible to start sorting things out straightaway," Joanna says. "Very quickly she got us sharing the problems and talking to each other. It was a real relief to know someone was there who understood us and our difficulties and could help us to find the way through the maze of our complicated life together. It didn't take us long to realise we really did want to stay together, and that there wasn't much we wouldn't do to make our relationship, and our blended family work as well as possible. Rebecca and Relate have a saying, which comes from a child psychologist who practiced more than fifty years ago. You just have to be 'good enough' parents, or anything else for that matter. You don't have to be perfect. Sometimes we were just trying too hard to make everything exactly right."

Karl feels that "gradually, since that second set of counselling sessions, our lives have settled into a pattern that works for us. The families have all come to terms with each other, and most of the tensions have gone. Not all of them. The perfect doesn't exist! We're a normal family after all. But everyone accepts everyone else and respects their views and opinions."

"Karl and I really understand each other. We have similar backgrounds and have had a similar upbringing. Our marriage, despite the difficulties, really works for us. To have stayed together after everything we've been through, we must have a lot going for us," says Joanna.

Karl says, "In the end, we know we made the right decision. How many couples stay in an unhappy relationship? Neither of us was prepared to do that. For all the difficulties we've faced, we wouldn't want it otherwise. Yes, we do argue sometimes. We're two different people sharing our lives. But we needed some help to stay on track and we have Rebecca and Relate to thank for the fact that such skilled support was there for us."

Joanna is nodding her agreement as Karl says that. "In the end, Cinderella did stay with her prince," she says, laughing.

A PROBLEM WITH INTIMACY

Shelley

"There was no sex involved, it was just a close friendship, not more."
That's what my husband said at our first meeting with Jill the counsellor. What is it with men? Somehow they think if you don't have sex it's alright. He'd tried to tell me that before, but I wouldn't accept it. Then when I finally got him to see a Relate counsellor he was trying to persuade her! To be honest, I was glad we had a woman counsellor, although she did say later on, when I said what I'd been thinking, that the men counsellors would have understood that too.

'Can you say what you mean by close friendship, Paul?' Jill asked him when he said it.
She said it really nicely, but I could see he was surprised. He tried to explain. 'Just started with talking about my feelings, she was sympathetic, seemed to understand me.' I wanted to interrupt him there and say 'what about me, I'm your wife aren't I?' but I didn't. I decided I'd let Jill do the talking.

Paul

It was true that my relationship with Sara didn't involve sex. She had a husband and wouldn't go that far. If I'm honest, if sex had been on offer, I might have taken it, but I am telling the truth when I say it never went that far. Most of the time we just talked. Neither of us was entirely happy in our marriages. She said Pablo – he was Spanish – was completely wrapped up in his job, which involved frequent trips to Spain and Argentina, and he was away for weeks on end. A lot of our communication actually was through email, and that's how Shelley discovered about it. I wasn't happy that she'd gone into my iPhone and found our emails, and some texts as well. It felt like she was intruding on my privacy.

So when Jill asked me about close friendship I told her honestly what it was like. Jill came back saying that we must have kissed because there was something about kissing in one of the texts. I didn't deny it had happened, but that wasn't the main thing. It was more about sharing our unhappiness and supporting each other.

Shelley

"Don't you think, if things were that bad, you should have been talking to me," I said. "After all a marriage is about sharing, and you were doing that with someone else, instead of me."
He didn't have an answer for that. It was at that point Jill began asking us about our marriage. The basic details she already knew as we'd been to an assessment session, but now she wanted to know about the emotional side and how things had been through the years.

I said we'd met when we were quite young. I was 18 and Paul was 20. We had a great time together and married two years later. That was 24 years ago. We were very close for most of that, and the sex was good. We've got two daughters, and Paul was very helpful and caring when they were young. It's only in the last four years or so things have gone downhill.
"Why do you think that is?" Jill said.
I didn't really know. Just something had changed. I said it felt like I was in 'free fall', like everything was going down and I had no control over what was happening.

Paul

Didn't it occur to you it might have been like that for me?" I said when Jill said that. I didn't quite know what she meant by 'free fall', but that feeling of being out of control was how it was for me too. At that point the first session had come to an end. Jill suggested we talked about that between us if we could and then come back to explore it more the following week. We both agreed.

There's a pub just up the hill from the counselling centre, and I suggested to Shelley we went to get a drink before we went home. Our girls are both in their late teens and perfectly capable of looking after themselves, so she agreed. Even said she'd drive home if I wanted a pint or two, so we went up there and over a drink we talked about that 'free fall' idea.

Shelley

"You should have told me you felt like that too," I said.
Paul claimed he didn't have any real idea that was how it was until he talked about it with that woman.
"But why her? Why not me?"
"It wasn't easy to talk to you."
"I don't understand that," I said, "we always talked for ages, before. Why not now?"
"We're talking now," he said.
"Yes, but it's taken a Relate counsellor to make it happen. "How do you think I felt when I found those messages on your phone?"
He went silent then. Just looked away and drank his beer. I tried to open up the conversation again but he wouldn't. Just shrugged me off. All the communication we'd done when Jill was there had dried up again. I knew then that without her we wouldn't be getting anywhere.

Paul

That week between the first and second session was really difficult. I'd promised not to contact Sara again, although I did send her an email to say what had happened. I felt really quite isolated. The girls have both got boyfriends. They spend their time with them and don't really talk to us. I found myself thinking about what Shelley said about being in 'free fall'. For me it was feeling really bad, like being trapped. I needed something more and I couldn't get that with Shelley

A couple of times during that week she tried to get me to talk, but I just felt as if I couldn't. She accused me of being stubborn, but that wasn't right. It was just so long since we'd talked and it wasn't going to be sorted that quickly. Both our girls noticed, which was quite something in itself. We hadn't told them we were going to Relate. 'You two are right mardi,' Helen the older girl said. She was probably right, but it wasn't just a bad mood. I suppose I really did feel like some kind of outcast then. It was like I didn't really belong any more. In the end I was surprised I actually wanted to go back and see Jill again. It felt like a kind of hope for something I couldn't sort out by myself.

Shelley

At the start of the session Jill asked how we'd got on during the week. I had to tell her things hadn't gone well.
"I try to talk to Paul," I said, "but he won't talk. Just goes silent. Like I don't matter any more. Like he doesn't want to talk to me."
He tried to say that was unfair then, but it was how I felt. Surely if I feel it, it has to be real.

Jill asked him to say how it felt to him if he thought that was unfair. He just said he couldn't talk to me at the moment. Something about me not letting him, which wasn't true. It was at that point she said something about there being no rights or wrongs, but that we had to accept each other's feelings and work from there. As soon as she said it, I realised some of where we were going wrong was there. We weren't *validating* each other's feelings. That's not my word. It's what Jill said, and the more I've thought about it since, the more true it's seemed.

Paul

When Jill said that about needing to validate each other's feelings it was like a window opening. I knew immediately that was what I didn't get with Shelley. She just wasn't accepting how things were for me. Looking back on it now, I can accept that was why I needed to go to Sara. She did validate my feelings, it felt like they mattered. But at home it wasn't happening. Even the girls thinking I was mardi wasn't treating me as if what I thought mattered enough.

And when I said all that, I knew Jill was listening to me. It felt like she understood and she was making Shelley understand too. But then she got me to see it was two sided. I wasn't allowing for how Jill was feeling when she said she was in 'free fall'. That was really her way of saying more or less the same thing.

Once we'd reached that point, we had to look back on all the things that let us slip into that position. Like me working hard and not always having time or energy for Shelley. Like her being naggy and not thinking I really cared, which wasn't true at all. I do care. When I said that, she tried to say it was true until Jill reminded her about the validating thing.

Shelley

We both had to accept some hard things in that session. It wasn't easy. There were times when it felt like she was on Paul's side, but I know that wasn't true. Afterwards I actually told Paul that and he admitted he's felt at times like it was two women against him, but he also accepted that wasn't fair. Our drink after the session, when he was happy for me to have a couple and for him to drive us home – another first! – was very different from the week before.

"Do you miss talking to that woman?" I asked him at one point.

If he'd said no, I wouldn't have believed him. He actually said he did a bit, but it was how it had to be. I knew that had to be honest. When I looked at him across the table I saw for the first time in ages the man I first fell in love with. Like all the ageing fell away and he was there again aged 20. It made me cry a bit. Paul wanted to know why and I told him. I think he was a tiny bit tearful then too, but he wasn't going to admit it.

After that session, we saw Jill another four times. I have to say what she did for us in just six sessions was amazing. We've got our marriage back. And it's as good as it ever was in bed. I think I'd have to say we're really intimate again. And to think, if it wasn't for Relate we might have divorced. I'm so glad we went.

Paul

Shelley's shown me what she's written. I don't disagree with any of it, not even the bit about me being tearful! All I can say is, I'm really glad we went to Relate too. I don't see Sara anymore. We both agreed it wasn't good for either of us. And the amazing thing is, I don't feel I need her. So it's a happy ending for me as well as Shelley. Thanks Jill!

Jill

Counselling Shelley and Paul was a privilege. They're a lovely couple and they responded very quickly to the things I put to them. I know that after just six sessions their lives have changed for the better. They came to Relate before things had got too bad to fix. I wish everyone did that. It's better and far less costly than ending a marriage!

DATE NIGHT

A story in four parts

Part 1

"Get home early tonight – date night, remember . . . ."
Lisa stood at the front door and waved as he drove off. Was that a tease, setting him up for later, or was there the hint of a threat about it; 'get home early tonight or else.' It was hard to know.

Jason waited at the end of the road to find a gap in the stream of rush hour traffic. Just as he was about to pull out, some idiot from the other side got there first. He jammed his fist down on the horn. A bald headed driver already in the line of traffic thought it was for him and lifted a forefinger violently.
"Piss off!" he shouted, but he was too late. The elderly woman in the next car stared looking shocked. At least it made him grin to himself.

It was a slow journey all the way to the office and by the time he'd parked the car he could feel the blood pulsing in his head. Missing his step in the revolving doorway and staggering inelegantly through didn't help, especially when the receptionists laughed. He signed in ignoring their greetings and stomped up the stairs to the first floor.

"Hi Jay, how's life?"
"Don't ask!"
"Bad as that?"
Rachel was peering up at him through her glasses. He tried not to stare at the low cut dress and its contents but they seemed to jump out at him. He could feel the anger inside shifting, like suddenly changing gear.
"Anything I can do to help?"

Was that a leading question? It was hard to be sure.

"Tea would be a good start," he said avoiding any complications. For now.

She turned, smiling, and walked towards the tea bar at the far end of the office. He followed her with his eyes. ' She'd be some date night' he thought.

*

"Next job, go home and clear up the wreckage!" Sian said.

The playground was clearing rapidly as the children bustled their way into the classrooms.

"Me too," Lisa said, waving pointlessly at Tom who had already turned his attention to the five year old world inside the classroom. It was still hard to believe both the children were at school now. At least it did give her some space to sort out what Sian had called the wreckage. . . and the pile of ironing and the next load of washing, and clean the bathrooms. . . It felt endless. So easy for Jason; all he had to do was get in the car, leisurely drive to work and stay there as long as he wanted. Was it deliberate avoidance when he got back late . . . sometimes just in time to play good daddy and read the bedtime stories . . . and sometimes not.

Inside the house again, the task seemed enormous. The local newspaper someone had dropped through the letter box was on Max's scooter still parked in the hall. So much for Jason's clearing up. Was all this the end result of ten years of marriage? She took the paper through to the kitchen, made herself a black coffee and sat down to glance through it before starting work. Page after page of charity events, football news, crass letters and photos of aged couples celebrating 'fifty years of happy marriage' stared out at her. She could feel herself grimacing. Eleven might just be a year too far for her.

An advert caught her attention: 'Relate the Counselling People'. She stared for a moment before pushing it aside and sipping at the coffee.

But the thought stayed with her. Before getting up she entered the number in her mobile; just in case. An insurance in case of need. You never know. But tonight was date night. Her idea of course; an attempt to get him home at a reasonable hour, maybe even reignite some romance. Two weeks ago he'd made it and, well, at least there'd been something. Too quick, but better than nothing. Last week, no show, not even in time for the boys' bedtime. She sighed. Their younger selves stared out from the photo on the shelf beside her. Where had all that gone?

*

It was just past five. Most of the staff were getting their things together ready to go home. Jason could too; except he didn't really want to. Most of the time now Lisa bored him; and Rachel said she was staying late. Whether it was an invitation or not wasn't quite clear, but he wanted to find out. He could still get home for 'date night' as she called it, put the boys to bed, avoid another scene. Probably there would be something on offer, although it did feel like she was throwing herself at him.

What might be on offer from Rachel felt altogether more exciting, maybe because it was less certain.

"Excitement of the chase, mate, that's what we need," his friend Neil said. He didn't seem to find too much trouble getting into women's beds.

"How many have you actually had, Neil?" he'd asked in the *Royal Oak* one night.

"Too many to count. You won't catch up with me." Neil said, laughing noisily as he took a large gulp from his pint glass.

Jason knew he wouldn't catch up. Apart from Lisa he hadn't started.

The office was largely empty when Rachel came across to him.

"My flat's just round the corner. Thought you might like a little something before you go home; if you want to, like."

He could feel the excitement rising inside him. His voice croaked for a moment before he could answer.

"Thanks Rachel, I'd like to."

"How long will you be?"

"I could finish now really. This can wait."

He put the document in his drawer and locked it smiling.

Her place really was just round the corner. It took almost as long to climb up to the third floor as it did to walk to the building. She turned the key and let him in.

"You'll have to excuse me. I'm not very tidy."

It was true. The bedroom door was open and he could see what looked like a pile of ironing by the side of the bed. In the living room where he was standing there were books and papers everywhere. His eye was drawn to her copy of *50 Shades*. He picked it up grinning.

"Is this good?"

"Depends what you like," she said.

*

The supervision session over, Tanya went back to the staff area for a break before starting counselling. Three sessions awaited her; two ongoing couples sandwiched by one new appointment.

"Go alright?"

"Yes, fine. Just needed to talk over a bit of over involvement. You know me; want to sort out everything."

Margaret laughed. Her rouged face seemed to get even wider. Tanya couldn't imagine anyone not liking her. Clients were lucky to get her, but she knew Margaret shared her problem. Knowing how easily you got drawn into the clients' lives didn't necessarily protect you from doing it.

"It's not always a bad thing." Margaret's gaze was on her. It felt like an invitation to say something.

"I know," she said, "But a failed marriage definitely makes you more vulnerable."

"Why do you say that?"

"Feels like I have to sort it out for others."

"Mmm." She didn't sound convinced. "Must go now, looks like my client has arrived."

Margaret guided her sizeable body through the door. Her green dress managed to resist the pressure from within.

"Nothing left for us any more is there?" Steve had said.

Tanya knew he was right. They'd barely communicated for months. Afterwards she discovered there was another woman. Instead of coming home after work he'd been staying late in the office with her. Eventually she realised parting brought relief, but the experience felt like it had left a legacy: the desire to help other couples work their way back to relationship. Mostly it was a strength. Sometimes it got in the way.

She looked at her notes again. Supervision had confirmed she was probably leading the young couple in the right direction. There really was a way forward for them. But before she had much time to think about it, there was a noise outside the door. Her next clients had arrived. She greeted them and took them through to the counselling room.

*

 It was seven thirty. After some grumbling and half-hearted resistance the boys were in their pyjamas and ready for bed.

"Where's daddy?" Tom was pouting. "He said he'd read me a story."

"Late as usual," Max said.

"He'll be home in a minute, you'll see," she said reassuringly without really believing it.

"Fat chance!"

"Max! Don't speak like that about daddy."

It felt like the right thing to say, but she couldn't stop herself smiling.

"What's a fat chance, mummy?"

"Don't listen to him Tom, he's being rude."

The smile turned to a glare at Max. She knew really he'd picked it up from her, but she didn't want him talking like that.

Tom had tipped his train set pieces out on the floor again. He turned back towards it and began constructing the circular track. Max was sitting on his scooter in the corner making fierce cornering sounds with his mouth as if he was driving a fast car in some American movie.
"Just five more minutes and we're going up. Don't get too carried away."
Neither of them acknowledged what she'd said. No surprises there, but she knew she meant it. Anger building inside her. The last thing she needed was one of the boys to push her over the edge.

She looked at the clock. Already ten minutes had passed since her announcement. It was becoming obvious Jay wasn't going to make it.
"Right, that's it," she said. It came out like a threat, which wasn't really what she intended.
"Told you," Max said.
"Told me what?"
"No show. He hasn't bloody made it!"
The words seemed to light a fuse in her head.
"Max! How dare you talk like that. Go up to bed now. Straight away!"
Tom looked up surprised. As she glared at Max, already retreating through the door, out of the corner of her eye she caught his grin.
"And you too! Put those train bits away immediately."
"Oh mum . . ."
"No arguments. Right now!"
Only the sound of the train pieces clattering back into the box broke the icy silence.
"Up!" she said once he'd finished.
Meekly, Tom made his way through the door and his feet pattered up the stairs.

There was no sound from above. She sat down and as quickly as it had flared the anger subsided. In the corner of her eyes she could feel tears forming.

Continued on page 87

THE FIRST VOICE

Relate is about providing counselling to people who need to talk – find ways to work through their difficulties – and it's therefore perhaps the role of the counsellor that first comes to mind when thinking about what we do: a skilled person, calm and kind; a quiet room, private and safe; the process of beginning to unburden, to share, to heal . . .

But before you even reach the comfort and safety of the counselling rooms, you must make the call to our reception team, a dedicated bunch known as "First Voice" because it is they who will take your initial call – often hesitant, sometimes fraught – and talk you through the options available.

Making that first call is never easy. It takes courage to move from the private pain of accepting there's a problem to the point of doing something about it. It takes strength to then speak to a stranger, a disembodied voice in fact, and explain why you need help. Even just vocalising the situation is enough to trigger emotion and our First Voice staff often find themselves on the line to tearful callers. They know just how to deal with these calls. If you've ever been that person, crying on the other end of our phone line, you'll know this already.

Our First Voice team members receive training which gives them a solid understanding of the potential emotional state of our callers and the techniques to deal with calls sympathetically and helpfully. Many First Voice receptionists come to work with us because they *want* to be in a caring environment, working for an organisation that's helping others. Thus they approach each call with that willing mind-set: they *want* to help, they *want* to be part of the healing process by easing the making of that initial call, organising an appointment to suit you, and providing a welcoming environment when you arrive for that first counselling session.

The First Voice team take confidentiality seriously. Their room is a designated "quiet zone" to avoid background noise disturbing conversations with callers. They file, store and archive client records under strict security, and they respect the privacy of our clients. First Voice staff truly enjoy their role in the counselling process.

And one thing our First Voice team love is seeing clients, several sessions on, emerging as happier, more confident people who are glad they took that brave initial step and called Relate – and who are appreciative that when they did, they reached a Voice that guided them through the process of making an appointment with efficiency, understanding, kindness and respect.

Afterword 1

There's honking and shouting from a car stopped at the lights as I walk past. A young man and woman are gesticulating. When I look at them, I recognise a couple I counselled a few months back. The gesticulations turn into thumbs up signs. They're both grinning.
"We're still together!" the man shouts as the lights change and they drive off.
I can't help smiling as I carry on with my shopping.

VIEWS FROM THE COUNSELLOR'S CHAIR

TEN HOURS TO CHANGE THREE LIVES
A family problem

I had a headache at the end of my first family session with Zena and her parents. It was like being on a battleground between sixteen year old Zena and her dad. They simply couldn't agree about anything, and underneath was a smouldering resentment. And perhaps beneath that, a desperation to put things right between them they just couldn't manage. Poor mum was in the middle of it all.

I did manage to get something of dad's history. A former soldier, when Zena was eleven, he'd been involved in a fight. He wasn't the cause of the problem, but a sudden violent incident at a regimental occasion left him bruised and with kicks to the head. He hadn't provoked the problem, just tried to help a mate, but the outcome was what we call PTSD, post-traumatic stress disorder. It's something soldiers often get from war zones, and it can have a serious effect on victims' lives. In Zena's dad's case it had left him with a persistent feeling of anxiety which meant he was on alert most of the time. It also caused a very short temper, something which hadn't previously been part of his character. His behaviour easily became aggressive and he shouted a lot, which was a problem he didn't really recognise himself. All that came out in the difficult first session. At least I knew the score!

My challenge was to create enough calmness in the second session so the family members could actually grasp what they wanted each other to hear. Mum was able to tell dad how much she thought he'd changed. He'd lost a fairly senior job in the retail industry just as he was building a new career out of the army, and was now employed in a lesser role on the shop floor. He was resentful and felt none of it was his fault. Worse, it had all undermined his self-esteem. Zena's relationship with him had been affected and she couldn't understand what had happened. During this session she was also very direct. 'I hate you,' she told dad. It was obvious he was shocked, but it was something he had to hear so he really knew how serious the situation had become.

By the next session the family dynamic had changed. Zena was angry now because it looked like mum had changed sides. Mum was seeing things from dad's point of view, and it was something Zena was determined to resist. It was time for some tasks. I wanted them:

- To speak to each other without swearing
- For each family member to remove themselves from the situation if they could feel they were getting angry
- For Zena to try to avoid anger in her responses

In the following session I asked them to score themselves on a scale of 1 to 10 and then to share their score with the other members in the family. Inevitably there were disagreements, and other problems emerged. Mum was treating Zena in a babyish way, maybe in compensation for the difficulties with dad. And underneath all the anger, Zena seriously lacked confidence in herself. By now dad was changing. He was trying to control his rages, but still struggling and defensive. By the end of this session it was beginning to feel like we were making real progress. Not everything was solved yet, but all three of them were trying to understand each other and communicate.

The seventh session was a real turning point. In counselling, there's frequently a point at which the way forward becomes clear. So what was different? I could see in this session that mum, dad and Zena were all really talking to each other. There was a magical moment too. Zena wanted to hug dad. Surprisingly, she asked my permission first! I looked at dad's face. It was obvious how much he wanted it. And you can imagine how willingly I agreed.

We worked together for three more sessions. These sessions felt like a consolidation of what had happened in that crucial seventh session. Dad had really softened his whole way of being, which made it much easier for mum and Zena to interact with him. All the anger within the family was dissipating. By the time we ended, it felt to me as if they really would be able to keep the changes we had worked towards. Of course, like in all families there will have been problems to face. But they had the tools and the understanding now to work their way through arguments.

When I think back over family stories, it never ceases to amaze me how quickly massive changes can take place as soon as the family members start really listening and talking to each other. I'm sometimes called a referee by clients. It's often true at the start, but I know I need to move out of that role as soon as possible. They have to take responsibility for staying civilised themselves. When that happens, there's always a way forward.

FINDING A WAY THROUGH

Sometimes clients come who seem stretched to breaking point. That's how it was with Ben and Rachel. They were both in their forties and had come to Relate on the recommendation of their doctor. When I first met them I could sense immediately how exhausted they were; with each other, with life, with circumstances beyond their control? At that point as counsellors we don't know. The first task is to find out as much as we can from the two perspectives in the room. And they're often very different.

One of the earliest questions I ask is 'why have you come for counselling now?' Ben and Rachel knew. It was because their older daughter Charlotte had got engaged.
"She looked so happy when she told us," Rachel said.
"We were really pleased," Ben said.
"That's lovely," I said, or something like it, wondering why something happy could trigger a visit to relationship counselling.
"Seeing them together, both 21 and planning their life, we could see how they loved each other," Ben said.
"And it's not like that for us."
As she said it, Rachel looked across at Ben. Client chairs are always separate but adjacent, turned half way towards each other. The small gap between them in my eyes at that moment seemed to grow. But as counsellors we've all learnt not to jump to conclusions. This just felt like there was more than a couple simply growing apart.
"You see, we have another daughter. Emma. She's 18. . ." Ben stopped, like he couldn't go on
"We really love her," Rachel said, "but she has multiple disabilities."

Gradually it came out, although it felt as if they were struggling to admit how difficult it all was. Emma was wheelchair bound. She had to be carried everywhere. She couldn't speak. It was hard for her to communicate what she wanted and because of her limited mental development she often didn't know what she wanted or needed. Rachel didn't work. Emma was her life. Their only income was from Ben's job, which was tiring and demanding. Both of them were exhausted most of the time. Respite care was limited and had also since the recession been significantly cut. The daughter they loved had become a burden. It was like all roads out of the impasse were blocked.

Talking about Emma didn't come easily to them. They'd been married 24 years but both had come from families where personal issues were rarely discussed. This was at first a barrier. Even between themselves they talked very little about Emma and the problems she caused. Both had slotted into a pattern of relentless caring. Their daughter had come first and they didn't regret that, but the effect on them as a couple was obvious. One of the first tasks of counselling was to encourage Rachel and Ben to talk about feelings. And gradually they began to open up.

Both felt the loss of intimacy between them. They each knew it had gone, but couldn't discuss it. And intimacy meant the whole range of personal interaction from basic touch through to their sexual relationship which was rare and no longer carried the excitement and closeness it had during the early part of their relationship.

We had just reached the point when Ben and Rachel were beginning to address these more difficult areas when Rachel's father died suddenly from a stroke. Both had been very close to him and really felt his loss. It was suddenly very important to help them to cope with their feelings of grief. This was really important in itself, but also helped both of them to express their feelings further. Gradually, without minimising the sense of loss they felt, we moved back to looking at how they might regain the intimacy between them.

And then, through her school, Emma was offered a residential weekend away. This was to be an assessment to see if she might be able to benefit from a place in a residential college. There were many complicated feelings aroused with this. We had to talk it through. They felt guilty that Emma would be going away from home, and anxious about how they, and Emma, would cope with this. Always before they had veered away from talking about her future. It just felt too painful. Now they could not avoid it. The session was probably the most emotional of all 15 sessions I had with Ben and Rachel. But when they came back to see me a fortnight later, they'd made the decision. Although not able to understand much, Emma had been able to let them know she was happy about the residential weekend and they had agreed.

The weekend fell between our next two sessions and when I went out to greet them in the waiting room for our session I could see immediately something had changed. They looked really relaxed and happy! It did not take long for them to explain why. Rachel had booked them a weekend in a remote farmhouse in Norfolk. They'd not done much exploring in the area; most of the weekend had been spent in bed. I don't think I said this, but in my head, I decided it was a crash course in intimacy! Counsellors have feelings too of course, and I just felt like getting up and dancing round. I'm sure they could see how happy I was for them.

After that, it felt like most of the counselling work was done. All that was needed was to help them learn strategies for maintaining the progress. We had two more sessions and then after a gap a further session to review progress. The difference between the first and last session was amazing. Rachel and Ben looked happy, were willing to talk about their feelings and seemed well able to develop their own lives despite the continuing care that Emma would require from them. They were missing Rachel's dad, but able to look forward to Charlotte's wedding.

Counselling is not about telling people what to do with their lives. The heart of counselling involves working with people and helping them to find ways forward that are right for them. I like to think that's what I was able to do for Rachel and Ben, and perhaps, from a distance, for Emma too. The feeling I get personally when I can do that is very special.

THE OUTCOME ISN'T ALWAYS WHAT YOU EXPECT

George and Sarah were in their late thirties when they came to see me. He was very tall, with deep set eyes, and she was glamorous, with long blonde hair and obviously attractive. They looked an ideal couple who might almost have been featured in a glossy magazine. But I soon discovered communication between them had deteriorated to not much more than functional and each felt under-valued by the other. Sarah had a friend, Platonic she insisted, but he was someone she had a personal connection with and who she admitted she could talk to more easily than with George. In the first session this wasn't presented as a key issue, but George clearly resented the relationship. 'A stumbling block' to progress in their marriage he thought. Both of them appeared to share the same goal. 'We want to get our marriage back to how it was when we first wed', Sarah said, and George agreed.

They had two daughters, aged nine and seven. George said the relationship between him and Sarah had deteriorated since the birth of their second daughter. Sarah wasn't so sure this was right. Both were adamant that they loved their daughters and didn't blame the girls for anything. But it was clear that family life was centred round their needs.

I sensed there was a need to give more specific identified time to their personal relationship and towards the end of the first session I raised this as something that they needed to consider. But it takes commitment and determination. It involves moving backwards from the functional communication patterns which have become established and which have become unsatisfactory for both partners. This was what I explained at the end of the first session.

During the second session we explored how the improved relationship might be achieved. We discussed dedicating one hour a week when they would both escape from all other distractions and spend time with each other. Their personal relationship would be the focus during this hour. Both George and Sarah seemed keen on this idea and went away saying they would find an hour from their busy lives.

However, when they returned for the next session they hadn't found the hour we'd agreed. There were apologies of course; protestations about busy lives, work commitments, spending time with the girls etc. They were so apologetic I felt like a critical school teacher as we explored all this in some detail. By the end of that third session both of them committed once again to find the hour. But still it didn't happen. The fourth session was in some ways a repeat of session three. I was beginning to feel that a real commitment to the relationship was lacking.

When for the third time George and Sarah failed to find the time to work together on their relationship it became clear to me we needed to look at things differently. I asked them to consider three different patterns:

1. They could choose to stay together with their relationship unchanged. That would involve accepting it as the way of the future.

2. They might finally find a way to undertake a renewed commitment in another way and move forward as a more united couple.

3. A separation, even if briefly could provide an opportunity to reflect on their relationship and what they each individually wanted from it.

The options were sobering for George and Sarah as we discussed what could happen next. Both felt option 1 was unacceptable. Equally option 2 had proved impossible to achieve, at least at the present time. The inevitable consequence was that option 3, radical and challenging, might need to be considered.

We explored separation seriously. Neither wanted to say that permanent separation was the right solution. But a temporary split, offering time for reflection, time to try out being apart to see how they each felt was a serious consideration. They left the session to consider their options carefully in their own time.

It was three weeks before I saw George and Sarah again. I had to cancel one week, and the next week they did. By the time I saw them George had already moved out and rented a flat for himself. The children were with Sarah in the family home. They had agreed amicably how George would continue to spend time with the girls. It was very noticeable in the session how the tensions had eased. George said he missed being at home, but found the freedom of his own place liberating. Sarah, laughing, said there was less work to do and less mess without a man around the house. Both felt it was too soon to make any long term decisions about their relationship.

We had one more session after that. Neither of them was ready to make any kind of commitment to when they might get back together again. The existing arrangements were working well and there was a need to give it time to settle they said. I offered them sessions separate from each other, but they both declined this. Instead we agreed to book another appointment a month into the future, when decisions might be clearer.

That appointment was cancelled, and another made for a further month into the future. When they both came back, it was actually ten weeks since the previous session. George in particular looked very different. He was wearing a colourful shirt and a new pair of shoes. He'd grown his hair longer and was wearing a different pair of glasses.

The change in Sarah was less marked. She still glamorous and wearing a quite a short dress. 'How are things?' I asked. They looked at each other before answering. 'We're going to stay apart', George said. I wasn't entirely surprised. 'It's mutual?' I said. They both nodded, but it was a moment before either of them offered any explanation.

'You helped us to understand what we'd not been facing,' Sarah said eventually. 'When I think back on it, I half knew we weren't going anywhere when I first came to see you. I just hoped there might be an answer somewhere.'
'I was the same really, although I don't think I knew it,' George said.
'So was it a relief when I suggested you separated for a while?'
'I was scared at first,' Sarah said, 'but I kind of got used to it really quickly. It wasn't long before I didn't want him back.'
George is grinning. He obviously hasn't taken offence.
'How about you, George?'
'I like having my own space. I can still see the girls. They like coming over and staying.'
'They do,' Sarah adds, 'and it gives me a bit of freedom too.'
I was wondering if either of them had started a new relationship. George's appearance seems to suggest that he had.
'So it's all worked out well? No regrets?'
George is shaking his head. He seems entirely happy. Sarah looks less certain.
'It's quite hard after all that time together,' she says, 'makes me sad sometimes, but I'm OK.'
I nod and smile.
'George of course has found someone else . . .'
'Well not exactly . . .'
'You said you had . . .'
'I've got a new friend,' he says.
It's quiet for a moment in the room. George looks a little embarrassed, and Sarah avoids eye contact.
'So you've both moved on really,' I say.

It's not quite the end of the session in terms of time, but George stands, seeming to want to end the session. He stretches out his hand for me to shake.

'Thankyou,' he says, 'you've been great.'

Sarah is standing now, with her hand also held out.

'Yes, thankyou so much.'

'I hope you feel it's been worth it.'

'Oh yes, we've learnt a lot, or at least I have,' Sarah says.

'And me. A lot about ourselves really.'

I escort them to the reception desk and see them out. I watch them go. Outside our main door they stand together saying a few words and then move off in opposite directions. Even now it's difficult for me to say how I felt. Not all relationships survive. Helping couples to an amicable separation is something we can also achieve. I ought to have felt glad for them. But if I'm honest, there was also a feeling of sadness in me, and telling this story again now, I can still feel it.

Bournemouth. A hot afternoon on the beach: two faces are familiar. Surely not? Meeting former clients on holiday is a mixed blessing, but the woman seems uninhibited, rushing up to me in obvious pleasure, her call louder than the roll of the sea. Her partner follows up close behind. I recognise them both.

"You counselled us!" she says.

"I did!" I say. I know I did. "Five years ago?" I say tentatively.

They laugh.

"What is it, Jim? Got to be at least ten. It was . . . well you know," she says.

I do know. The embarrassed grin always means sex therapy. But Jim is looking smug.

Suddenly I'm aware of a boy of eight or nine running up to us and calling out.

"Look dad!"

In his hand is a small net, and in it something he's caught. The boy is not alone. Behind him is a smaller boy, closely followed by a girl of around four, and in her hand a toddler who looks like another girl. The four of them gather round us. Suddenly I remember. Judy and Jim. They look older but otherwise hardly different.

As Jim inspects the contents of the boy's net, Judy sidles up and almost whispers in my ear.

"It worked a treat," she says.

It takes a moment to grasp the meaning of what she says. Jim and the children have already run off along the shoreline.

"Must go," Judy says, and in no time she's sloping off in pursuit of the family.

The sun is shining brightly over the water as I walk on.

GETTING BACK TO INTIMACY

They look no more than 25, but Esther is conscious of a tired dullness about the couple she's ushering through the door room 3. It feels as if the life energy has drained out of them. Carmen's Southern European features have none of the voluptuous sparkle of her famous namesake, and Simon seems overwhelmed by the force of gravity. They sit in the chairs and look at each other. Esther smiles but doesn't immediately say anything. She lets the clients settle a moment and watch; allows the atmosphere of the enclosed counselling space to settle around them. You learn a lot that way she always says.

It's Simon, looking uncomfortable with the silence, who speaks first.
"We met at Durham. The university. We were both there together."
Carmen smiles, inclines her head forward slightly in agreement.
"We got into a relationship quite quickly," he says.
"Not long after freshers week."
It's the first time Carmen has spoken. She smiles and then casts her eyes downwards. It seems shy, almost embarrassed.
"I'd had a couple of girlfriends at school, but for you," he says, turning towards Carmen, "it was the first time wasn't it?"
"It was," she says.
Is that guilt? Esther notices. Don't make assumptions, she reminds herself. Wait to see what develops.
"So, talk me through it; how things progressed." It's the first time Esther has spoken since they've entered the counselling room.

The story is halting at first, and Simon takes the lead. It's a familiar story; sex driven romance developing a life of its own until their identity merges into an item. Simon sporty and outgoing, attractive to Carmen, who really does have a Spanish grandmother and has inherited her name. And it's Carmen's good looks and unworldliness that drew him to her. Much of the excitement is in the campus nature of their relationship. Parents, home life, familiarity have nothing to do with it. They're in another world, and another image. Simon and Carmen; everyone at uni knows they're an item, even the tutors. The investment grows through the first two years.

In the autumn of their final year Carmen meets Maurice and Sue, Simon's parents and stays for a long weekend. They like what they've heard about her. They like who they meet. There are hints about weddings, even grandchildren which is flattering. . .

"And a bit scary," Carmen says. "I remember that night. They'd done up a room for us. There was no problem that we slept together. But it felt very . . ."

She struggles for the word.

"You said you had a feeling of dread," Simon offers.

Carmen nods. "I did," she says. "And all that weekend we didn't make love. I just couldn't."

"Carmen's dread got to me too," Simon says, "it was both of us."

"What do you think that dread was about?" Esther asks.

They look at each other.

"I think it just felt . . . very domestic," Carmen says.

"Domestic?"

"That wasn't what we were about. It just felt . . . wrong really."

Simon is nodding. It's like he's understanding something for the first time.

"After that I felt I had to get Simon to meet my parents. We're not quite as posh, but I didn't think you'd mind," she says, turning to him.

"Of course not."

"Well they liked Simon. I knew they would. Mum was even flirting with him."

It's the first time there's any laughter. Simon makes a gesture of fanning himself and Carmen flicks him playfully with the back of her hand. He grins.

"She's very Spanish and outgoing. Much more than me. Julietta she's called. Well, they were as bad as Simon's parents, my dad as well, except more openly. Asked us about wedding dates and all that. Didn't bother to check with us whether it was what we really wanted to do."

"You stayed there? At your home with Simon?"

"Another long weekend."

"And . . ?"

Simon understands immediately what Esther is implying.

"The same," he says.

"No sex?"

"No."

They look across at each other and then down to the floor. An uneasy silence returns to the room. Esther waits, allows it to settle. This time it's Carmen who continues.

"We sort of fell into it. Before we really knew it we were planning to get married at the end of our studies. We're not really religious, but my mum and dad are Catholic."

"My mum and dad aren't catholic but churches are all the same to me so I went along with it," Simon says.

"We found ourselves agreeing to this big white wedding," Carmen says, "in June after our finals. I suppose we got wrapped up in the idea of it."

It's like they're on a roll now. The caution at the start of the session is gone and they swap the story between them. Esther lets them talk.

"Our friends were excited. It made it seem like a brilliant conclusion to our three years at uni. We invited almost everyone. Sue and Maurice told Simon they were happy to meet most of the costs."

"I'm an only child. They'd already invested a lot in me . . . seeing me through uni and that," he says.

"We never really talked about it. Everything was just, like, what everyone expected. If I'm honest though, there was somewhere deep inside me that felt trapped into it all."

"You never said that . . ."

Simon looks really surprised.

"I know. I sort of didn't really know it. Not then. Does that make sense?"

Esther is nodding. "Sometimes we can get caught up in things. Let ourselves go through with something because it's expected of us . . . like the wedding? So we can't allow the doubts to surface."

She looks from Carmen to Simon then back again. It's obvious they can understand what she's saying.

"We couldn't let all those people down," Carmen says.

There's silence for a short while.

"So . . . we got wound up with it all. I went for dress fittings with mum. You spent two nights in Paris on your stag night. . ."

"God I was wasted after that!"

They both laugh. For a moment the tension eases and Esther allows herself a smile too.

"Your hen do with that stretch-limo and all that fancy dress you told me about. That was just as bad!"

More laughter. Esther watches this time. A thought surfaces.

"Can you see what's happening?" she says.

They just look at her.

"How are you feeling right now?"

Puzzled looks have replaced the smiles. They look at each other.

"Well alright, I suppose," Simon says.

"Perhaps, in reliving it like this, the same thing is happening?"

"You mean . . ." Carmen stops. It looks as if something is beginning to make sense, but she can't say it.

"You haven't told me exactly why you're here. Are we escaping from what's real once more?"

Simon moves his hand out towards Carmen, touching her on the arm. It looks gentle, really caring. Their eyes meet, and she inclines her head towards him for a moment as if in assent. He turns back towards Esther.

"It's the sex," he says, "we don't do it now."

*

The sense of loss has felt like a weight in the room. But it's last session of the day. Esther completes her notes and locks them away.

"You look drained. Tough session?"

Melanie in the reception office smiles sympathetically. Preserving confidentiality is vital, but there are times when the chance to spill it all out would feel better. She shakes her head vaguely and smiles back.

"Want some tea?"

"No thanks. I'll get going. The walk will do me good."

"No worries. See you tomorrow."

At least it's still light outside. The evening sunshine always has a cheering effect. But Simon and Carmen are still in her head. All that planning for a perfect wedding; meringue dress, family bridesmaids, grandmother over from Seville, groom and best-man in penguin suits, the serious ceremony followed by the five course meal in a five star hotel, masking all those unspoken doubts. It's exhausting just thinking about it. Was it surprising they sat in the bridal suite afterwards and hardly spoke? What was it Simon said? 'It felt like a dark cloud had settled on me.' Carmen felt the same, but neither had shared the feeling. The wedding of the year, thousands of pounds spent, and both of them left with an overwhelming flatness afterwards.

The healthy physical activity from the early months of their relationship as they explored each other's bodies had dwindled to a sexless desert. But . . . and it felt like an important but . . . there was still a closeness. They could still relate to each other. Could all that early passion be rekindled? Like blowing on a fire that's close to being out, but you can still see the red embers. The comparison cheers her as she turns the corner into the railway station. The sun is directly ahead of her now. The sudden glare forces her to shield her eyes, but the sudden feeling of warmth is welcome.

*

When she collects them from the waiting area for the next session, there's an air of expectancy as they stand to greet her. Both of them have tentative smiles on their faces as they settle into the chairs and look across at her. This time it's Carmen who speaks first.

"You said we didn't talk about what was worrying us . . ."

Esther waits.

"When we were planning our marriage," she adds. "We've talked about that . . . since last week."

"Things were already slipping . . ." Simon says.

"Slipping?"

He looks at her. It seems as if he doesn't understand what Esther means. Carmen looks across at him.

"Our relationship . . . the sex," Carmen says. "We knew it wasn't all that good when we were planning. But we sort of put all our energies into the wedding. It was like . . . if we did that, the other thing would sort itself out."

"But it hasn't."

The energy seems already to have drained out of Simon when he says that.

"How much do you both want to stay together?"

They look at each other once more. The answer comes quickly from both of them, together but not quite synchronised.

"We do, yes."

It's what Esther had expected. She nods slowly. It feels like there's a need to allow the commitment to be absorbed not just by both of them but into the space around them.

"Then we've got some work to do," she says smiling.

"So, since the wedding, what fifteen months ago now, what has happened?"

"Well, after my degree I was planning to train as a teacher," Simon says, "but I persuaded myself I needed a better paid job."

"That's why you're working for the finance company?"

He nods.

"And it's going well?"

"I hate it."

He speaks quietly, but there's venom in his response.

"I tried to tell him he didn't have to do that, but it seemed to have something to do with his sense of being a man, the breadwinner and all that."

"I didn't say that."

"You didn't have to," Carmen says.

She sounds sure of what she says, and Simon doesn't argue back.

"And at this time, the sex wasn't going well?"

"It wasn't," he says.

Carmen clarifies; "He means there isn't any sex . . . between us, not for months now."

Somewhere outside, the alarm call of a blackbird penetrates the intensity in the room. Esther doesn't hurry to intrude into the silence.

"So you've both lived like you're in a flat share. No sex, and for you Simon, a job you hate. Marriage hasn't brought you that much fun has it?"

He doesn't answer. Again, he doesn't have to. The face, with grim disappointment etched into it, tells its own story.

"Does it have to be like this?" Carmen says.

"We always have choices," Esther says.

It feels trite, as she says it, but it is what she believes.

"I'm understanding you both want to change the whole basis of your lives. Get somewhere towards where you were when you first developed your relationship so that it's satisfying within the working lives you lead now."

"How can we do that?" Simon says.

"That's something we can work on during the coming weeks, if you're both really determined to do it."

They're nodding enthusiastically in front of her. It occurs to her that there's something more hopeful about them now as the session ends.

"Have we ever been like that?"

"What?"

Esther looks up. David is staring at her over his newspaper, a perplexed smile on his face. She grins back, feeling slightly embarrassed.

"Sorry, I was in my own world. Ignore me."

"Clients again?"

She nods. Sometimes it would just be good to share, but she can't. Confidentiality is just that. She can't share with anyone, not even her amused looking husband sitting on his usual chair reading about world events.

"I was just wondering about whether we've ever had a time when we just couldn't share things between us."

"What do you think?"

"God David, you're sounding just like a counsellor yourself!"

"Well what do you expect, living with one? But no, managing my own staff is quite enough thankyou."

He rustles the pages of the newspaper like a ripple of applause for what he's just said.

"Well we have talked over the years haven't we," she says.

He's smiling once more, probably wondering if he'll be able to carry on reading, or whether she wants to get into a complicated discussion about relationships.

"Nothing stays the same forever," he says, "we've had to work at our relationship, reinvent ourselves every so often, like everyone I suppose."

It amazes her how he can sometimes make simple statements that get to the heart of what she's thinking about. Of course it's true. It is what everyone has to do. Sometimes a relationship can feel like a camera going out of focus. What you think you see through your own viewfinder becomes distorted through time. So adjust the focus, take a fresh look and see if that helps. It's what she'll have to work on with Carmen and Simon. Radical refocusing in their case. Explore all the built up expectations and get rid of the dysfunctional ones. Move forward together in a relationship that really meets the needs they've got now.

David has disappeared behind his newspaper again. Escaped while the going was good and she'd returned to her inner world of clients. 'You worry too much', her supervisor says to her, 'shouldn't be thinking about it at home'. Which is true in theory, hard to keep to in practice, especially with people struggling like Carmen and Simon. She stands, walks across to David, leans over his newspaper and kisses him on the cheek. The surprise on his face makes her laugh.
"Thankyou," she says.
"What on earth for?"
Her first thought is to say it's for coming up with such a sensible thought. But it's not the whole truth.
"Thankyou for being you," she says. "I'll make you a cup of tea."
His bemused look makes her laugh.

She walks through to the kitchen, fills the kettle and plugs it in. While she waits, the dialogue with David becomes a monologue inside her own head. 'This hasn't just happened. We've had to work for our own middle aged intimacy. When it's gone out of focus we've adjusted. Refreshed it all.'
The kettle boiling noisily rouses her from her thoughts. She makes the tea and takes it through.

*

"So," Esther says once they're settled into their seats, "are we ready to talk sex?"
Their smiles are not entirely without embarrassment, but after a quick glance at each other, they both nod.
"Tell me about how it was when you first met."
"He couldn't keep his hands off me," Carmen says quickly with a grin.
Simon, grinning, doesn't disagree.
"And how long was that the case?"

They look at each other again.

"Well . . . I suppose right up till I met Simon's parents, like we've told you," Carmen says.

"You said something about that being too domestic."

They're both nodding.

"But if you want a relationship to develop into something more lasting, you have to make changes through time."

They're nodding once more.

"Can we explore why all that marriage planning left you feeling so flat?"

As she expects, there's a long pause.

"I think . . ." He doesn't finish, turning instead to Carmen for help.

"We were so involved in the planning, caught up in . . . well *having* to be so excited in the wedding and all that . . ."

"We didn't really talk about . . ."

"But just once in a while . . . didn't you just feel we'd lost something?" she says.

"This feels like . . ." he stops for a moment, as if trying to find a way to say what's in his head. "You know when you start using a muscle you haven't exercised before . . . it sort of won't work properly; that's what this is like."

"He means sex," Carmen's face twists into a wry grin.

"No, no, not exactly. What I mean is . . . We lost all that fun we had together. I sort of felt we didn't really share things in the same way."

"And there was all that revision for the finals too . . ."

"It felt like sex wasn't all that important anymore, we kind of . . . just did it."

"Simon!"

"It's true! Surely you felt that too?"

"Yes," she says after a moment, "I suppose . . . it felt like we'd lost something. It was just a chore, like something you ought to do."

"And then we just . . . didn't."

There's a long pause. The silence in the room has a heaviness. Esther looks towards them as they seem to absorb what they've just said. Neither speaks for some while.

"So our task," Esther says eventually, "is to start again . . . get back to the days of your relationship . . . before you started thinking about weddings and things, and rebuild from there.

"Can we?"

Carmen's dark eyes look up at her hopefully, almost pleading.

"You really want to?"

She looks at Simon, whose hand slips across to hers. She turns to him and smiles.

"That's where you start;" Esther's nod indicates the gesture. "Rebuild the intimacy."

Another silence. The change is perceptible, lighter in mood, more hopeful.

"Forget about sex, for now. Get to know each other again, like you must have done when you first met. Focus on what you really like about each other, and see what happens."

*

Esther is immediately aware of an obvious difference in both of them when they come for the next session. Carmen is wearing a short dress in light blue which stops short of her knees and the functional pony tail has been replaced by a sleek new hair style displaying just how long it actually is. Simon has well cut jeans and more stylish trainers. There's a lightness about them as they stand to enter the counselling room.

"Something has changed," she says when they're sat down in front of her.

"We decided we needed new outfits," Carmen says.

"We've been on a shopping spree," Simon adds.

"Well it certainly shows."

"And we've been doing what you said. Trying to re-engage with who we were before it all started to go wrong."

Simon is holding Carmen's hand. He looks across at her and smiles. Noticing, Esther smiles as well.

"And," she says, "the sex. No attempts to force that?"

Carmen smile widens into a grin. "I've been flirting outrageously," she says, playing with her newly long hair, "and I've let him kiss me . . ."

"But no more?"

"Not yet," she says.

Simon raises his eyebrows, but he's smiling too. "You won't keep that up for too long," he says.

"You don't know about that. You've got to work for it."

Esther is smiling now. "Seems like we've made some good progress."

"And we've made another decision. Simon's going to give up his job at the finance company and train as a teacher!"

"I wasn't sure if it was fair on Carmen at first. I'll get a bursary for training as a maths teacher, but it's not enough to live on. Mum and dad have said they'll help. But we're going to have to rely on Carmen's income for a year before I get a job."

"That's a great decision," Esther says.

"I'm earning a good salary working in HR, which I really like. It's not a problem for me. It feels like we're turning around our lives big time."

Carmen's dark eyes really shine in the artificial light of the counselling room. The Spanish inheritance is very apparent now.

Esther uses the rest of the session to explore ways of developing intimacy further, helping them both to find ways they can avoid slipping back into old habits and losing the progress they've made in such a short space of time. They're so receptive, and their relationship is so obviously rekindled, that the gloom from the first time she met them is almost a distant memory. At the end of the session, she feels the need to draw some threads together.

"We've had six sessions now, and you've both made great progress. I think it's true to say you've rapidly making your way back to intimacy. I'm thinking perhaps two more sessions?"

They're both nodding.

"Next week we review progress with that . . ."

Simon is smiling. It's clear how he's interpreting *that*.

"And in the final session look at the future."

It's agreed, and the session ends.

*

It's impossible for Esther not to think of Simon and Carmen as she drives home. It's easy to say don't get too involved with clients, much harder to achieve. Confidentiality is important, but not saying anything doesn't mean you don't think about people inside your head. There's a strong sense of responsibility in her, almost a need to help clients sort out their difficulties. It's something she has to watch, and talk about with her supervisor.

"You can't solve everyone's problems Esther," she hears Jean saying to her.

"I know you're right. But I like to do the best I can."

Now she's driving home with a sense of satisfaction that one of her cases, with two such delightful people as Carmen and Simon, is going well. Why not after all enjoy the feeling of success to counterbalance the anxiety when the way forward doesn't seem clear?

"You seem happy tonight," David says when she gets in.

"Mmm. You've noticed."

"Hard not to," he says, bringing her a glass of wine. "Good sessions?"

"Yes," she says, taking a sip from the glass, "one in particular."

"Well I'm glad to see it. Better than the angst you sometimes bring home."

"I'm not that bad, surely?"

David's eyebrows are raised, but there's a smile too.

"Cheers!" she says, lifting her glass to his. "To Relate."

His eyes roll upwards to meet the raised eyebrows as he finds his newspaper beside his chair and opens it. Esther grins and sits back smiling to herself.

*

"We're back to normal," Carmen announces at the start of the next session.

If anything, they're both looking even more young and attractive than the previous week. Simon has even changed his hair style and looks slimmer. He's smiling and looking smugly pleased with himself.

"Congratulations," Esther says.

For some reason they all think that's funny, and laughter bubbles over in the room.

"So all that flirting achieved its purpose."

"That's one small step for mankind," Simon says.

The result is a playful slap from Carmen.

"He's been saying that all week," she says, "thinks he's landed on the moon or something."

Esther waits for the excitement to settle before continuing the session.

"You remember at the start you talked about becoming too domestic. . ."

It takes a moment for what she's saying to register.

"You'd lost sight of what really attracted you to each other and become ground down by all the busyness of your lives."

"It's very different now," Carmen says.

"The challenge is not slipping back again. It can happen very easily."

Simon is nodding his agreement.

Esther resists telling them what to do. She draws out some strategies from them, wanting them both to identify ways they can spend time together which is not about domestic arrangements. And drawn out, they're creative, and prepared to talk about maintaining their renewed mutual sexual attraction.

"I wouldn't have believed I could talk about all this . . . before I came to you," Simon says towards the end of the session.

Carmen nods her agreement. "It's really strange," she says. "We can talk more openly about our relationship when you're here, Esther, than when it's just the two of us."

"But the aim is to give you the tools so you can do it without me in future. That's what all this is about."

They reach the end of the session. Esther is conscious they've agreed on just one more session.
She stands. Simon and Carmen stand too.
"One more meeting then."
"Do you think we'll be alright . . . without you I mean," Carmen says.
"Well unless you want a cardboard cut-out of me to put in your bedroom wardrobe . . ."
They laugh. There's a nervous edge to it that wasn't there through the session.
"Endings are never easy. But you'll be fine. One more week then?"
"Please."
They fix the appointment.

"They're a really nice couple," Melanie says, watching them go out of the main door arm in arm. "They look really different now, don't they?"
Esther smiles. Melanie is fishing, but her curiosity has to be managed.
"Bit of retail therapy works wonders," she says.
"I could do with a bit of that myself."
"Couldn't we all."
"Too right! You done now?"
"Yes. Last one this evening."
"You look happy."
"Why not? It's a lovely evening out there, and David's promised to make me a lasagne for tea."
"Wish I could get my other half to do some cooking," Melanie says.
Esther can't quite resist a Cheshire cat grin as she walks out with a wave.

*

"Last session then?"

"We think so, yes," Carmen says as they walk through to the counselling room.

"Time perhaps to look at how we got to where you are now, and how you can stay there," Esther says as they sit down in the familiar seats.

They both indicate their agreement.

"I've been accepted for a place," Simon says.

It takes a moment for Esther to grasp what he's saying.

"Teacher training," he adds, reading the incomprehension on her face. "I start in September."

"Brilliant. So you'll give up the finance job?"

"End of August."

"That's really cheered him up," Carmen says, "he's even more horny now!"

And surprisingly, as soon as she's said it, her face registers embarrassment. It only makes Esther and Simon laugh.

"I take it that means the problem you came with is now a thing of the past?"

There's no need for an answer. It's written on both their faces.

The session passes quickly. It's a lovely summer day outside, and it feels as if the warmth has entered into the counselling room with them.

"You can always come back again if you need to," Esther says as they come to an end.

"We can't thank you enough."

"You've been great," Simon adds, "thankyou from me too."

They shake hands and make their way out into the still bright evening.

For Esther the glow remains. She sits down a moment in the counselling room. She needs a minute or two to gather her thoughts. But her next couple are waiting; a first appointment. She's seen them looking nervous as they sit in the waiting area. There's work still to be done. When she's ready, she adjust the chairs, a habit she's adopted to mark a new client, and takes a few deep breaths. Then she steps out into the waiting room.

"Hello, I'm Esther," she says, "do you want to come through?"

They follow her into the counselling room.

DATE NIGHT

Part 2

She'd seen Mark and Jo for three sessions already, but it felt like they'd been distant in a way that was hard to grasp. Tanya knew she needed to engage them somehow. But the fourth sessions was often strangely the turning point. As she took them into the counselling room, it was for a moment in her mind that this might be the breakthrough session. She could feel tension from both of them. But the first few minutes, the same surface calmness was in the room.

"Sometimes I think I love him, but I'm not in love with him. Do you know what I mean?" Jo said, almost out of nowhere. It was certainly something new.
Tanya looked at her without responding immediately. Instead it was Mark who filled the silence.
"I don't get that."
There was something dismissive about what he said. Tanya waited.
"You never do get it do you."
Jo was suddenly vitriolic. Mark was visibly shocked by the response.
There was agitation in the room now. The coolness of the first few minutes evaporating.
"I wish I could explain it better, but you don't help do you," Jo said, turning towards him and staring.
"You can see what she's like can't you."
It wasn't a question Mark was asking – much more like an attempt to recruit her to his side and against Jo.
"What do you want me to see Mark?"
"Well, you know, talking in riddles, not making things clear. How am I supposed to know what she means?"
"What do you think Jo means?"
"No idea – like I said, can't make sense of it."

Beneath the petulance Tanya was aware of something else. Another feeling not being expressed. She tried to let it filter through her conscious awareness, and fear was what emerged. She could feel herself engaging now, like a jigsaw piece suddenly fitting into place. Mark was scared. But she couldn't just say that. He'd probably deny it and react against the suggestion of weakness.

"It feels like . . ." she began, then hesitated for a moment, wanting to get it right. "It feels like there's something there . . . something there that you really want to know, but can't quite . . . can't quite get at."

It sounded impossibly clumsy, but suddenly Mark turned towards Jo and blurted out at her.

"What I have to know Jo, what I have to know, is . . . ."

He stopped, and Tanya could sense tears somewhere close.

"Is there still a way forward? Yes or no?"

The last part came out as aggressive, but she guessed it was a defence against the feelings. And suddenly Jo was crying.

"It isn't as simple as that. You always want easy answers." The flow of tears stopped her continuing and she grasped at the box of tissues between them. "Mark," she said, through the tears, "Mark. . . . I do want this to work, really I do . . . . but you've got to try as well."

Tanya watched as Jo stretched out a hand towards him over the tissue box and Mark responded. He didn't cry, but she knew tears had to be close. She could see now there was probably a way forward.

*

"Well?"

It was nearer nine than eight when Jay let himself on and walked through to where she was sitting in front of the television.

"Boys in bed then?"

"What do you think?"

"Shall I go up and see if they're still awake?"

"Please yourself."

Lisa watched him hesitate, turn towards the door, then turn back again.

"It's date night isn't it," he said. It felt so ridiculous she didn't bother to reply.

"I'm sorry. Had to get something finished."

"Three hours of it?"

"Rush job. Boss wanted a report for a meeting . . . . tomorrow morning."

"I see."

"No Lisa, you don't . . . it's not like that . . ."

"Like what!"

"Like . . . like I was late deliberately."

"So what's this then? Accidental lateness?"

"Look I'm sorry, I wanted to get home . . ."

"So why didn't you?"

"I've told you. Boss wanted this report . . ."

She looked at him, standing by the door looking pathetic. Was this the man she wanted to marry ten years ago? It didn't really matter whether he was telling the truth or not.

From somewhere she was suddenly conscious of a different smell. It was faint, but it was definitely there. She moved closer to check it out and it was on him. A perfume . . . not his . . . another woman, she was sure of it.

"Report?" she said with as much scorn as she could put together, "Another woman. I can smell her!"

She was shouting now, but it felt uncontrollable. It was obvious he didn't know what to say, confirming her suspicions.

"So what did you do with her? Quick shag on the desk then?"

"No Lisa, it's not like that, really it's not . . . "

"So what is it like then? Tell me that!"

"I couldn't sleep."

Max's face was at the door.

"Sorry Max. It's alright. I was just a bit cross with daddy for being late home."

As she said it she couldn't resist an angry glance across at him and Max noticed it.

"Are you really cross, mummy?"

"I've been thoughtless," Jay said quickly before she could answer. "Come on Max, I'll take you back up to bed."

He grabbed at Max, lifted him onto his shoulder and walked out of the door. She heard his heavy step on the stair. It felt like a convenient escape, but she knew she couldn't leave it. There was an open sore now which had to be dealt with.

*

The session with Mark and Jo had felt like a break-through. And Tanya's final clients of the evening had come to a successful conclusion too. At least for now they'd made the decision to stay together and finish the sessions. It had been a good evening. She walked through to her tray in the main office before going home. There was a message for her. Would she take on some new clients to fill the space? Jill had drawn a little smiley face against the question mark. It made her smile; as soon as she did, she knew it had already had the intended effect. How could she refuse? There was a brief résumé: 'Woman rang – Lisa – distressed – thinks husband may be having an affair. Says he's agreed to come along too. Wants urgent appointment.'

Tanya could feel herself grimacing. How often did clients say it was urgent she wondered? Things had to have been deteriorating for months, if not years. Why not get in touch before it was urgent? But then . . . that wasn't what she and Steve had done; and now they'd gone their separate ways. Could a counsellor have saved things for them? Maybe. Would have been cheaper, and easier. Half a dozen Relate appointments didn't begin to amount to the cost of the separation. Oh well, it was water under the bridge now.

Her watch told her it was eight fifteen. Making her way back via the waiting room she came across an emaciated looking girl of perhaps thirteen sitting next to a well-rounded woman. The contrast was marked. The girl looked up and gave her one of those embarrassed half smiles that seemed to suggest a strange combination of shyness and desire to communicate. She smiled back. As she did so, Margaret came into the room and the girl and the woman stood in unison. Tanya couldn't resist a smile at the similarity between the adult shapes contrasted with the girl, but resisted speculating further on what the issues might be. The words 'eating disorder' were however irresistible.

*

Lisa was nervous. The friendliness of the waiting room didn't do much to alleviate her feelings, but at least it was better than the coldness she'd somehow expected. Jay, sitting next to her was silent. His jaw was compressed tightly and she wondered if he would actually say anything once they got into wherever it was going to take place. 'It' was frightening. She'd rung up on impulse and got the appointment before even asking Jay, lying to the woman who answered the phone and saying he'd agreed. It wouldn't have surprised her if he'd refused to go, but he'd half-heartedly said he'd go. Then she'd wondered if he would actually turn up in time, but again he'd made it. Perhaps the thought of her mother's accusing presence as she baby-sat the children had scared him into coming straight to the counselling centre.

From nowhere it seemed, a slim woman in a blue dress was standing in front of them.
"Is it Lisa, and Jay?"
"Yes," she said quietly, her voice almost breaking with the anxiety of it all. Jay just stood up and nodded curtly.
"I'm Tanya, your counsellor. Come this way."
The corridor to the counselling room was dark, but the walk didn't take more than a few seconds. Tanya indicated where they should sit and she found herself next to Jay, with a lamp and a box of tissues on a small table between them. 'I'll probably need those,' Lisa thought to herself before turning and smiling nervously at Tanya, who smiled

back. The blue eyes and well groomed blonde hair made her think for some reason of a British Airways flight attendant.

"Thankyou for coming, I know this can't be easy," Tanya said.
"No." She looked at Jay, who seemed to be staring at the wall beside him, almost as if he was trying not to be there.
"I need to ask you a few basic questions first. Is that alright?"
She nodded and noticed Jay did too. It didn't feel like saying no was an option. Children, status, length of marriage, which Jay got wrong, saying twelve when she knew it was ten years, and so on. There were legalistic bits too, which didn't seem to quite make sense. Then eventually the bit she was dreading.
"So that's done. Can you say now what problems you might be experiencing? Who wants to start?"
She looked at Jay, who looked back at her blankly. Neither of them spoke.
"It doesn't matter how you say it," Tanya prompted, "Any order, just as it comes."
Lisa realised she was going to have to start. No way he was going to.
"Well we tried this date-night idea," she began.

"Date night?"
Tanya looked across at Jay and Lisa. The body language was familiar. It reminded her of Jo and Mark. Another man struggling to cope with feelings. Steve too. That was what he was like. But don't generalise, she reminded herself. Every man's struggle might look similar, but inside they were all different.

She found herself staring at Jay as she said it, almost willing him to respond.
"It was Lisa's idea," he said, looking across at her as if he wanted her to explain.
"You can tell me if you want to," she said, "what was it like for you?"

Before she could feel embarrassed by what she'd said, Jay grinned. He'd picked up the unintended suggestion. It was the first time he'd shown any emotion and she found herself warming to him.

"I don't quite mean it that explicitly," she said smiling herself, "just the general idea."

"Well, I kept getting in late from work. Lisa didn't like it."

She glanced across at Lisa. Was she close to tears?

"This date night thing meant I had to get home in time to see the boys to bed. Then it was our time, like."

"Did it help?"

Before Jay could say anything more, Lisa interrupted, her eyes flashing with anger.

"Once! That was all."

"No Lisa, more than that . . ."

"Once!" she said again with an air of finality.

Looking across at her, Tanya wondered if the anger might dissolve into tears, but it didn't. She just sat there looking away from him.

Tanya could feel the hostility in the room. But it felt alive, something she could work with. Dissipating it too soon might be a mistake.

"So it hasn't really worked then?"

There was no reply from either of them, but Lisa shook her head slowly. She could feel the sadness and for a moment she almost felt like crying herself. But something else too; the feelings in the room didn't tell her the relationship was finished. There's hope here she decided, I can work with these two.

*

It was already seeming like a bad idea; coming back for the second session. The first one had been hard work. Now it was happening again. If Lisa was going to shout him down like that, what was the point? Two women against him. How could that ever be fair, but probably this counselling thing wasn't something blokes got into.

"Did it seem like a good idea to you at the time, Jay?"

It took a moment to focus on what Tanya was saying.

"Date night you mean?"

"Mmm"

"Yeah. It was alright I suppose."

Lisa was staring at him. She'd be shouting again in a moment.

"No better than that?"

"Well I did want us to get together again."

"Together again?" the counsellor said.

"Yeah."

She was looking straight at him, as if expecting him to say more.

"What are we talking about Jay?"

She was still looking at him when Lisa spoke again.

"Sex he means. It's all he thinks about."

"No Lisa, that's not fair . . ."

"Isn't it?"

"Well it's not all me. It used to be good, before Tom."

"Remind me, how old is Tom?"

"He's five," he said quickly. The impulse to turn accusingly towards Lisa was strong, but he managed to resist it. Then Natasha or whatever her name was said it for him.

"You mean sex hasn't been right for the past five years?"

It surprised him that she could be so direct. But she had understood. He nodded and looked down at his hands. It was suddenly hard to look outwards.

"Are you blaming that on me?" Lisa said. He could feel the sharpness in her.

"Well you don't ever seem to really want it," he said.

"You just don't understand do you?" Lisa said. It was typical; always blame it on him.

"What are we talking about here?" The counsellor was looking straight at him again. Did she expect him to spell it out? Then Lisa filled the gap, which strangely felt like a relief.

"I wasn't well after Tom was born. I just didn't want it for a while, but he didn't get that. Always trying to force himself on me."

"That's not fair!"

"Isn't it? And now it's you who doesn't seem to want to get close anymore. Sometimes I wonder if there's someone else."

*

Tanya wondered when an affair would be mentioned. But Jay's response didn't emerge in words straightaway even though his eyes stared at her indignantly. He was almost bound to deny what she said, but there was some kind of guilt there too. Not her job to quiz him though. Just be there, allow things to develop; stay in the moment she reminded herself.

He looked almost surprised when she didn't press him on it; and Lisa seemed disappointed. How often counselling with couples felt like being cast as a judge. But she knew she had to resist it.
"Would it be surprising if there was?" he said eventually, but more coolly than she'd expected.
The answer felt evasive, but that pause, was it guilt? She wasn't sure.

Lisa was staring at him now, looking almost as if she wanted to attack him.
"Is it true then?" she said, almost wildly, "*is* it?"
Almost without warning, the anger seemed to collapse into uncontrollable tearfulness, like she was pleading with him.
"No Lisa, no, it's not true," he said, putting out his hand towards her.
At first she resisted, arching her body away from him. Then as if the tears and the reaction had melted his defence, there were tears in his eyes too. He stretched his hand out again and this time she held onto it with both hers as if he was some kind of lifeline.

For some while they sat there in front of her holding each other. She waited. Jay was the first to move.
"Sorry," he said.
She nodded without saying anything straightaway. Lisa too seemed to emerge from some place deep within herself.
"You do mean that?" she said to him.

"Yeah," he said, "there's nothing."
"You've not slept with anyone else?"
"No Lisa, I swear to you."
It looked like the truth.

Continued on page 123

RELATE GOES TO SCHOOL

One of the most important activities for Relate is the work undertaken in schools. Beginning initially in secondary schools, this has been called Relateen. However the service now extends to primary age children. Counsellors spend agreed time within the host schools, who manage referrals of children identified with needs, or who ask to see a counsellor. The accounts that follow are from school staff, counsellors and the students themselves.

VIEW FROM A PASTORAL TEAM LEADER

When our headteacher agreed to having a Relate counsellor in the school I was really delighted. Then I was a bit anxious because the room we had for her was only tiny, not much more than a book cupboard and with no window. I really wasn't sure it would be good enough for counselling. But when Gill saw it she thought it would be fine. 'It doesn't have to be big,' she said, 'sometimes the small space is helpful for talking about difficult things. It's more intimate'. The smile on her face looked genuine, she wasn't just trying to be nice. When she put it like that it made sense. The absence of windows would help confidentiality too.

We agreed I would manage the timetables and the weekly referrals. The head had agreed to pay for three hours a week. Gill said she could see four children in this time, with 45 minute appointments. It didn't take long before her appointment timetable was full. I soon realised a lot of our students needed more than one session, so there had to be a waiting list. And that list grew alarmingly!

Gill has been working with us now for a whole term. During that time she's seen 11 students. One girl has had eight sessions, but most have been shorter than that. The average is about four sessions per student. One of the problems we've had to face is that students generally don't want others to know they're seeing a counsellor. We try to manage that, but it isn't easy.

The other thing we've had to work out is the amount of confidentiality that needs to be preserved. As head of the pastoral team I have responsibility for the wellbeing of all the students. I know who goes to see Gill, but mostly I don't know why they go. For me, and also for other staff, we tend to think we should know professionally if there are problems. We have agreed that tutors will know if a member of their group goes to see Gill, but the reason will not be disclosed. Only if a student approaches a tutor or anyone else saying they need to share what's happened in their session can a discussion begin. Some staff didn't like that, but we've all accepted it.

There are of course some things the counsellor has to disclose. Basically they involve situations where someone is at risk of harm. There's a legal requirement to report sexual or physical abuse. This is explained to students at the start of their counselling sessions. We haven't actually had any disclosures like that so far, but we know it's always possible.

The students who have received counselling so far have all told me it has helped them, and tutors say they've seemed more settled in school. Next term we've got the GCSE exams, and there's one lad who will definitely do better as a result of Gill's work. He tells me counselling has 'freed' him. A couple of students have been prepared anonymously to share their stories and I know they feature in this book. Some of our most troubled students have been really helped. The next challenge for me is to persuade our head to find more money to increase the number of Relateen counselling hours we have . . .

HENRY

Sometimes he just wanted to talk about his play station. It was like a relief from the big stuff that we talked about in and amongst his day to day existence. 'Human kind cannot bear very much reality' the poet T.S. Eliot says somewhere and it's true. Children especially need to cope with the most traumatic things in small chunks. Their growing selves might be distorted by too much too quickly, or even too soon.

Henry had a lot of reality to bear. He was ten when he came to see me. His twin brother had been killed in a hit and run accident outside the school. It had shocked everyone and several youngsters needed counselling support. For Henry it was a much greater need. His parents and his older sister were grieving too. He needed space for his own feelings and help to understand.

I knew what had happened before he came to see me for the first time. So I didn't need him to spell out why he was struggling. Gently I could tease out his feelings of grief and help him to understand in a straightforward way what was happening to him as he worked through the various stages of grief. Elizabeth Kübler Ross's five stages of grief may be half a century old now, but they still provide a very understandable outline if what we all have to go through when faced with loss of any kind. The loss of a twin brother is so vast, an initial stage of denial is inevitable. Talking in the first sessions about Archie, his brother, as if he was still around was a clear indication that was where Henry still was. My first task was to see him through that stage.

It was also when the pattern for the ongoing sessions became established. With a little over half an hour each week, after an initial welcoming I tried to bring out how he was feeling. I soon got to know when Henry couldn't take any more. He had ways of letting me know. Usually it involved an abrupt change of subject to something he was doing. A film he'd watched maybe, something from school, or the ubiquitous play station. I always allowed that. Sometimes there was an opportunity to spend a further five minutes focusing on his feelings about Archie towards the end. And sometimes he would initiate it himself. 'What do you think happens to people when they die?' he asked me once. I gave him a kind of non-committal answer and then asked him what he thought. 'I don't know," he said. Then after a pause, 'But they're not here any longer are they.' There was a sharpness in his response which indicated to me that he might be moving through into the stage Kübler Ross called the angry stage.

That was confirmed the following week when he came into my room noisily and let the door clang shut behind him. His face was set firm, and his look almost intimidating. 'The driver is going to be in court', he said. The headteacher had already told me that, but I let him tell me the story in his way. Unusually, he focused almost the entire session on his rage at the driver. I sensed tears might not be far away, but everything was channelled through anger. Only at the end did he talk about a girl in his class who had annoyed him in an argument about a pencil.

In the few sessions following, Henry showed occasional flashes of anger, sometimes directed at other children in his class, and occasionally at me. 'Has anyone ever died in your family?' he once asked. When I said yes he seemed surprised, but let it pass without seeming to want to know more. He began one session with the statement 'He's got five years'. He was referring to the driver. The tone of his statement implied what lots of people thought; it wasn't much for the loss of his brother's life, but he didn't spell it out.

There's a third stage according to Kübler Ross. She called it bargaining. It's where a grieving or a dying person tries to bargain in order to stave off the inevitable. I didn't see a lot of that in Henry, although he did once want to consider what might have happened if he'd died instead of Archie. It resembled what we call 'survivor guilt' and is something else that often has to be faced by those who survive tragedies where others have lost their lives.

There's a fourth stage; depression. From personal experience I know this is in some ways the hardest of all to cope with. Anger and bargaining still involve fight against what has happened. It's what Dylan Thomas called the 'rage against the dying of the light'. Depression, by its very name, is the stage beyond that, when the fighting is done and loss is recognised for the awfulness it really is. During this period, Henry would frequently come in and sit within himself in his chair and not want to say anything. We spent minutes in silence. It didn't feel uncomfortable to me; I sensed it was something he just needed. There were three cancelled appointments at this time. I assumed he just couldn't face coming in and talking with me.

That stage seemed to last for ever. If I thought that, what was it like for Henry? It was then he wanted to talk about his play station toward the end of each session. He talked about something called *Resogun,* a programme he had on his PS3. It seemed to be quite a violent game and I wondered if it was the angry stage returning. Although we talk about the stages progressively, they certainly can interact with each other and moving backwards and forward definitely does happen. More likely, he just needed the grounding of the game, and whatever others he had on his PS3.

I got glimpses into his family during this time too. His mum seemed to be experiencing depression too from what he said, while his dad carried on working and I don't think talked much about his feelings over what had happened to Archie. He never talked about his sister even though I asked him occasionally. His class teacher talked to me. She was worried about him and thought he wasn't recovering from the grief. I explained the process to her and I think it helped her to understand.

The accident had been in November. By this time we'd almost reached the summer holidays. In September he would move on to the secondary school. Fortunately, Relate also works in that school, so I could keep up the continuity. Via his teacher I made arrangements with his mum to see Henry a couple of times at our counselling rooms in Shrewsbury. It was something he seemed happy to do. Between these two sessions the family went on holiday, a week that also include Henry's eleventh birthday. The break seemed to have made a difference. He was smiling when he came into the counselling room and wanted to tell me about what he'd been doing.

It felt to me like he was on the edge of moving into Kübler Ross's final stage of acceptance. The hurt and sense of loss hasn't gone, it never will. But there's a recognition that it's possible to move on with life. We actually talked about Archie during this session like he was a wonderful brother that Henry had been blessed with. That was his word, although he might have picked it up from someone else. 'All good things come to an end', he said. Again, I guessed he'd got that from somewhere and asked him who else thought that. He said it was his mum and dad. They seemed to have had a talk with him while they were on holiday. Most important was the fact that the words really did seem to reflect how Henry was feeling. I asked him if he would like me to come in and see him when he was at his new school and he said he would.

As it happened, we only had two more sessions. The more positive mood from the session in Shrewsbury stayed. The excitement, and the inevitable reorientation involved, probably also contributed. We agreed he could contact me again if he needed to via his form teacher and ended the session. It felt quite emotional to me. At the end I shook his hand and he thanked me for my help. I didn't see him again.

Working with Henry was one of the most challenging counselling assignments I've ever undertaken. At the same time, it was also one of the most rewarding. It really did, and still does feel like I helped him to move on with his life. It felt like the essence of what counselling is all about.

AMY

When Amy first came to see me she couldn't look at me. She just lowered herself into the chair with her hands clasped protectively across herself as if she was sulking. Her school uniform was scruffy with the tie knotted untidily around her neck with the narrow end trailed down and held in close to her chest by her arms. The form I've been given by the school staff says she is 13 and has 'troubled relationships' with other girls.

As is usual for me, after a brief 'hello,' I wait before saying anything else. Amy doesn't respond to my welcome. Eventually, I say 'hello Amy, I'm Jim, how can I help you?'
For a very brief moment her head lifts and dark eyes stare at me from within half closed lids before quickly dropping down again.
"They keep picking on me," she blurts out into the space beneath her.
"They keep picking on you?"
Again, the head rises briefly and the eyes flash at me as if to say 'I've told you that already.'
"Who is picking on you, Amy," I say.
"Tracey . . . and Joanne and Tyler . . . and that . . ."
Her voice trails off. There's a pause. I wait.
"They won't stop," she adds after a while.
"Do you tell anyone?"
"They don't believe me. Say I cause it."
"Who is . . ."
"Teachers, all of them," she says raising her voice and cutting me off.

It's an impasse I've reached before. In my former life as a teacher, I've met other Amys, struggling to find a way to relate to others and getting grief as a result. In the old days, teachers tended to ignore the problem, telling victims like Amy to 'stick up for themselves'. A few could, and fights sometimes followed. Many couldn't, and suffered their whole school lives. It's not how we respond now. We try to help, with counselling for those like Amy who can't find a way out of their difficulties.

But I can't make assumptions. Every victim is different. I need to know more.
"So Amy, tell me in a bit more detail what happens."
"Call me stig and things," she says.
And much worse I guess.
"And you want them to stop."
She nods, but there's no sign of any belief that I or anyone else can do anything about it.

Gradually we talk through more detail and I begin to suggest some survival strategies. But it feels like this is too soon. I need to do more work on building her trust in me first. I start asking her about her family. She's the youngest of six children. No dad. Living quite a harsh existence with very little money. She tells me mum doesn't work, and they have to use the food bank in the town.

By the end of our first session she's been able to look at me more often and the defensive arm position has loosened.
"Do you want to come back next week?" I say as we reach the end.
"You won't tell no-one?" she says quickly, her face suddenly fearful again.
"We agreed, didn't we? Confidential."
She nods.
"But I want a promise from you."
A puzzled look comes over her face.
"Who's your favourite teacher? The one you can best talk to?"
Still with a surprised look on her face, she names a young French teacher, Miss Davies, whose name has come up in sessions with other youngsters as being sympathetic.
"If you have serious problems this week, you'll tell her?" I say.

Amy doesn't answer straightaway. Then cautiously, she nods.

"And is it alright if I tell her we've made this agreement?"

There's sudden anxiety again in her face.

"Just that? No more?" I add.

I'm anxious now. She just looks at me without any response. What I don't want is to leave her vulnerable during the forthcoming week without any possible support. After quite a pause she nods. It's no more than a brief drop of the chin and a momentary closing of her eyes, but it's enough. We end the session with a reaffirmation of her commitment to come back again next week.

At the end of my morning appointments, I seek out Miss Davies. I'm cautious in what I tell her, wanting to keep my own promise to Amy, but she catches on straightaway.

"I feel sorry for her," she says, "I'm so glad you're working with her."

"Just in case," I stress, "the most vulnerable time is often when there's a change."

She seems to understand.

"Thanks, Miss Davies."

"It's Laura."

Amy's second session arrives. She's late, and after almost ten minutes I start to worry. When she does come it's a relief.

"Got kept behind in maths," she says, sitting down in the chair with a very audible clonk.

Involuntarily, I smile. She notices, and a sly grin crosses her face. It's reassuring and an indication that a connection is building.

"So how's it been this week?"

"Same," she says.

But she's looking at me, and her arms aren't tight across her chest.

"Any big problems?"

She shakes her head but doesn't say anything.

"Name calling, that sort of thing?"

"Yeah."

There's resigned sadness in the one word reply.

Laura has told me one of the problems is Amy's inability to resist responding to taunts. We've both agreed it needs to be stopped, but if I can help her to manage herself better, and someone from the school talks to the key culprits of what is after all a form of bullying, things should begin to improve.

First, I need Amy's agreement. She's reluctant at first. Received wisdom says asking for help will only make things worse.
"So what can you do to improve things," I say.
"Nothing."
"Nothing at all?"
She shakes her head despondently.
"Why do you think they pick on you?"
She shrugs her shoulders. Years of suffering are in that shrug. I wait.
She looks up at me, and surprisingly, keeps the eye contact.
"You don't understand," she says, before looking down again.

For me that was a low point in my work with Amy. I knew what she said was true. I haven't had an underprivileged background, I haven't been bullied. School wasn't a problem for me. But I had established a connection with her, and I was going to keep it. Sometimes in counselling the difficult moments offer a way forward.
"Help me then Amy. Help me to understand."
Once more the shrug.
"One thing that might make a difference."
She doesn't reply immediately. I wait. Beyond the door to the small counselling room I'm conscious of voices passing. Someone drops something and there's a swearword. It's like a prompt.
"What do you say when they start?" I say.
"I tell them to fuck off!"
"And what happens?"
"They laugh and say horrible things."

"What might happen if you don't respond?"
Another shrug.
"Is it worth a try?"
No response.

I let the silence grow in the room before speaking again.
"Can I ask Miss Davies to talk to them?"
"No."
But there's a pause before she says it, as if she's had to consider the idea. Once more I wait.
"Worth a try? You do your bit, and Miss Davies does her bit?"
Again there's no immediate response. But sometimes you can just feel things moving in the silence. I take a risk.
"Deal?"
She looks up at me. I can see a mixture of hope and fear in her eyes. This has to work I tell myself as her head moves forward into the slightest of nods.

I ask her the names of the girls causing the most problems. I know she's already told me, but I want to be able to pass them on accurately. Then we spend the rest of the session working on strategies for staying cool next time there are any taunts. I sense hope growing inside her. But I know it's a lot to ask.
We finish the session. There's a cautious smile on her face as she turns to say goodbye. I have another child to see, and when I finish that session I go to find Laura Davies.
"I'll see what I can do," she says.
"What do you think the chances are?"
"A lot depends on what you can do with Amy."
"I know," I say, "I'll do what I can."

Every so often during that week I thought about Amy. I always try not to, but some clients just have that effect on me. So in some ways it's a relief to see her again. And something about her manner gives me hope.

"How has the week been?" I say.

"Alright."

From Amy, that sounds really positive.

"So no problems?"

She shrugs, but it doesn't look negative.

"No one's said anything to you?"

There's the faintest of smiles on her face. It feels like a good start. But there's work to do still. If we have made progress, slippage is always possible, even likely.

During the next month I have four more sessions with Amy. We have just one set-back. Just one person makes an unpleasant comment and she responds in the old way. But that's told to me as just something that's happened by Amy. She's had the courage to tell Miss Davies, and she sorted out the problem.

During the last week of term we have our seventh and final session. Laura has already told me how changed Amy is now. Staff report she is more attentive in lessons and it seems like others no longer want to make fun of her. I knew from my own observations week by week that her confidence was developing, but a counsellor in one room inevitably doesn't see the whole picture of day to day interaction within a large school. Laura's confirmation helps a lot.

"So how are we today then?" I say.

"Much better."

It's really a significant difference; positive, and said with a smile which I can only replicate.

We consider how things are different, and why. I tell her I think the important things include owning up to the problem, letting the school help and learning to control her own responses. She says the girls who have made life difficult for her have changed too. She's even developed a friendship with one of the girls previously on the edge of the taunting. All this takes place as a calm discussion and it's hard to remember just how defensive she was at the start of our sessions. We finish. I tell her it has been really good to work with her. There's a coyness and a blush as she says 'thankyou' before looking down with embarrassment. By the time she reaches the door she's recovered her composure and turns back to wave at me with a gentle smile on her face, and for the first time I get a glimpse of the woman she will become.

I've carried on working at the school since those sessions with Amy four years ago. I can't say every session has been as productive as those seven sessions, but staff have told me many of their troubled youngsters have benefitted from counselling. This September Laura handed me a card in an envelope addressed to 'Jim the counsellor'. It was a thankyou card from Amy. Inside I read that she's gained nine GCSE passes, two with an A grade, and seven others at grades B and C. She also tells me she's now at the sixth form college and has a boyfriend. The work of being a counsellor can have unexpected high spots even after the work is finished.

Afterword 3

Mutual healing

A year ago I needed an operation. It's a strange and unsettling experience. You lose consciousness with the anaesthetic and the next thing you know someone is calling your name in the recovery room.
"Annie, Annie," I heard.
I opened my eyes and a blurry face was looking down at me.
"All over. Everything has gone well."
The face coalesces into a recognisable form. Suddenly, it's familiar.
"Lucy?"
"Hello Annie. Yes it's me. You healed me. Now it's my turn to heal you."
I smile
"But not to think about that now. Just rest. In a short while we'll take you up to the ward."
I slip back into drowsiness.

Some hours later Lucy visits me in the ward.
"How are you?"
"I'm fine," I say.
There's a grin on her face.
"How many times did you tell me not to say that?"
I'm smiling now.
"It's very British isn't it!"
Lucy is still grinning as she checks my wound.
"Yes, everything is fine," she says pointedly.
"And how are you now?"
"I'm fine too, thanks to you."
I start to say something else, but she stops me.
"Please. Just rest now. Maybe tomorrow we can talk."
She's smiling, but the voice has determination in it.

I watch her walk through the curtained area surrounding me. Before I drift back into sleep, the memory of counselling her and her husband is in my head. I settle back contentedly despite the soreness from my wound.

HELEN

I'm 15 and in Year 11. My dad left home a long time ago and I live with my mum and my brother Jacob who is 12. Two years ago, mum had a stroke. Her left arm and left leg have been badly affected. She can only walk slowly, dragging her leg behind her and she can't really use her left arm at all. We've got Jean, a social worker who helps mum with things, but I have to do lots of cleaning and washing and that. I also look after Jacob and make sure he gets to school.

As well as all that, I have to do my school work and I take my GCSEs in the summer. I want to do well as I want to go to university and be a solicitor, but it's really hard to get everything done. I can't go out much with friends. They've stopped asking me because they know I won't be able to come. It upsets me when I see on Facebook how everyone has a good time at weekends and I'm stuck at home looking after mum. I don't blame her, but I get upset about everything.

When Mrs O'Reilly asked me if I wanted to see a Relate counsellor to talk about what things were like for me I didn't know how that would help, but I said yes anyway. In my first session with Lorna the counsellor she just asked me to talk about what things were like for me. She's lovely and easy to talk to. It took a while to say exactly what I felt like. It seemed strange because most of my life now I have to think about mum and Jacob. I cried a bit when I was saying it. I don't really know why, but Lorna said it was alright. When that session ended I felt drained, but better. It was really nice that someone wanted to know how I felt.

Friends asked me what I'd talked about. Lorna told me that would probably happen. She said no one would know from her as it was confidential. I could say what I wanted, but if I didn't want to say, just tell them she'd said I shouldn't. So I didn't. What happened felt like it was my thing and no one else's.

In the second session, Lorna asked me if I was angry. I said no I wasn't. She just looked at me when I said that. I didn't like her asking it. After all it wasn't my mum's fault she got ill. We talked a bit, and after a while I realised I was a bit angry. Not at mum, or even Jacob, but because it seemed unfair. Lorna said that was normal. It surprised me, but it felt good admitting it. It was something I didn't think I had a right to feel and she said I was suppressing it. Again it felt better just being allowed to say it.

I had six sessions altogether. They all got me to feel like I mattered and I was allowed to have feelings of my own. Lorna also helped me to find time to do my homework and we worked out schedules. More than anything, Lorna helped me to feel like I wasn't abnormal. Sometimes it's embarrassing having to do what I do. No one else I know has to look after their mum, but Lorna says there are lots of us all over the country. She put me in touch with a young carers website, and I've made contact with other young people like me. I've discovered getting angry is normal too, and Lorna has helped me to understand why. It might seem strange, but knowing I'm allowed to feel angry has meant I don't get angry so often.

Lorna's counselling has been great. I tell my friends online how good it is, and at least two of them have Relate counsellors in their schools too. I tell them to go and talk. It's really worth it.

ADAM

When I was in Year 10, I discovered there was a Relate counsellor working in our school. Mrs O'Reilly announced it in assembly. But we couldn't just go to the counsellor's room. We had to see her first if we wanted an appointment. I thought about it, but didn't want to tell Mrs O'Reilly. It took me a month to decide to see her, and when she asked what it was about I said 'Something personal miss.' She looked at me for a moment and I wondered if she'd insist on knowing, but she just nodded her head and said OK.

It took another three weeks before I got the appointment. I was really nervous when I went in. The counsellor said her name was Gill and asked me to sit down. 'How can I help you?' she said. I didn't answer at first. Then I said 'It is completely confidential isn't it miss?' 'You can call me Gill you know', she said. Then she said that if what I told her didn't mean me or anyone else would be caused harm by anything I said, it would be completely confidential. I remember saying 'that means you won't tell anyone?' She nodded her head, looking directly at me and said 'yes, it really does'. She has very dark eyes and looking directly at me and it felt as if she was trying to see right through me. But I did believe her. She seemed really nice.

So I started. I'd practiced what I might say in my head, but it didn't come out how I'd planned it. I just said 'I keep wanting to kill myself.' She was very calm, like it was alright to say that. She didn't say 'you mustn't do that', or get angry with me for wasting her time or anything. Just asked me if I'd tried to do it yet and how it felt when I had those thoughts and other things. I said I hadn't tried yet. She wanted to know if I had any plans about how I might kill myself and I said no, they were just thoughts that came over me.

Then she asked me why I wanted to kill myself. It was the question I was waiting for. I just looked at her for a moment not knowing how to say it. She just waited, like it was OK to take my time. Then it was out.

'I think I might be gay,' I said.

It came out quickly and I couldn't look at her.

'How do you feel about that?' Gill said after a moment.

'Bad'

'And that's why you've been thinking about suicide?'

I nodded.

That felt like a really important moment. I'd not admitted my fears to anyone before. Once or twice I've been called gay, but everyone gets that. I've even said it to others. But it was a relief to be able to be able to tell someone who just accepted it. Gill didn't criticise me or tell me I was wrong. She just helped me to talk. Over the next two sessions I told her how I never really fancied girls, but was interested in other boys. I said there were times in the changing rooms when I'd been scared I'd get a hard on and really had to stop myself looking at boys when they were naked. I knew really when I told Gill I thought I *might* be gay it wasn't the whole truth. I actually by then *knew* I was gay.

In the third session, Gill asked me what I wanted to do about being gay. 'Did I want a relationship' she said. I said I did, but it was scary. She wanted to know why, and I said I was scared of being found out. I was also scared of actually having gay sex but I didn't tell her that. I think she guessed though. She wanted to know if I knew any other gay lads. At that time I didn't. She just nodded when I said that. 'You will,' she said, 'when you're ready.' That felt good. Like it was permission to stop worrying and take my time. I actually remember relaxing into the chair and her smiling at me.

The next thing Gill wanted to know was whether I was ready to tell my mum and dad. I wasn't. I think that was what I was most worried about. But I said I thought I could tell my sister. She was 18 at that time and studying for her A levels. At first I didn't know if I wanted to do that. Gill said think about it, and if I did want to, we could talk about how I could do that in the next session. During that week I kept looking at Holly, that's my sister, and trying to imagine how she might react. Once she said something about me keep looking at her. Of course I said I wasn't, but I knew she didn't believe me.

But by the next session with Gill I'd decided I would talk to Holly. Gill let me talk to her about what I might want to say and how to find the right moment. She also wanted to know if I thought Holly would keep it to herself. I thought she was the only person I knew I could trust enough, so I got myself all psyched up to do it. And when it happened it was a lot easier than I expected. When I told Holly she just said 'is that all? I thought you'd done something terrible the way you wanted me to keep a secret.' 'You think it's alright?' I said. 'It's still you isn't it? We're all different. Anyway some of my best friends are gay.' Then she gave me a big hug and promised she wouldn't tell anyone. 'That's up to you,' she said.

That evening, after Holly knew, I felt so relieved I can't tell you. Every so often Holly looked at me and smiled. It was like a secret communication between us. I'm pretty sure mum and dad didn't notice. I knew I wasn't ready to tell them. I went back and saw Gill the next week and she was really pleased for me. We only had one more session after that. We agreed I'd probably done as much work with her as I could for the time being, but she said I could come back if I needed to. Before we finished, she asked me if I still had any thoughts about suicide. I didn't. I was ready to live my life.

I'll never forget how important Gill was to me. Now I'm at sixth form college studying for A levels myself while Holly completes her degree this year. I've come out at college . . . and I've got a great boyfriend! Everyone sees us as an item. I never imagined that could all happen. A few weeks ago I told mum and dad. I did it when Holly was home from uni as I wanted her support. In the end I couldn't believe how OK they were about it. Even dad gave me a hug and said the same sort of thing

Holly did when I first told her. I think he said 'you're still my son,' or something like that. It made me cry it was such a relief.

So thankyou Gill for everything you did. You were my life saver in lots of ways. If there's anyone reading this with a worry like I had, go and see a counsellor. It could save your life too.

THE HEAD'S TALE

If I'm honest, I was very sceptical when Tracey our young teacher responsible for welfare and safeguarding first put the idea to me. Buy in a Relate counselling service for the school? What for? I grew up in a tough mining village in South Yorkshire. My dad spent his life working down the pit. There were problems enough there, but we didn't talk about them, cry on each other's shoulders and all that. We just got on with life. What benefit would there be for our children to spew their emotions all over the carpet. And we weren't that well off as a school. Why throw away funding on some counselling project. If anyone needed a talking to, wasn't that what our own staff were paid for?

But Tracey's very persuasive, and very good at what she does. There aren't many staff who could have got me to talk to some woman from Relate telling me how much they could benefit my school. Well there were two of them that came. One was a smartly dressed colourful, slightly alternative looking woman with smiling blue eyes and short blond hair. She called herself the chief executive. With her was a smaller younger woman in a black dress with long dark hair. They were very presentable, but I couldn't help thinking my Year 11 lads would have them for breakfast. I'd never appoint either of them as teachers.

I wanted to know what advantage Relate could bring to my school. The counsellor asked me if I cared about the children who had problems. It made me angry for a moment. Of course I do. They all matter. Everyone of the children in this school is important. But I don't think she meant any harm. I think she just wanted to suggest there were ways they could help that I couldn't. I didn't find that easy to accept. In some ways I still don't, but I have to admit there have been some significant changes in some of our children since they've had counselling.

For a start, those youngsters who had real home problems; dads who have left, financial difficulties, young carers and quite a few others, they've all had real support from the counsellor. And they do seem to respect her too. Then there are the behavioural problems. Relate were keen to tell me they weren't running a service to improve the behaviour at my school. I wouldn't have believed them if they had. But some of those the counsellor has seen who did sometimes cause behavioural problems don't any longer. I suppose it's obvious really; lots of poor behaviour, low level disruption, horse-play, that sort of thing, comes from a need to be noticed because they don't get that at home. Or worse. With a counsellor understanding them, they get their bit of individual attention from someone who helps them manage their behaviour and find better solutions.

The thing that has most surprised me is the effect on exam performance. Our GCSE results have improved since we brought the counsellor in three years ago. A lot of that of course is the work of our hardworking teachers. But we've tracked a real difference in the performance of those who have had counselling. More settled, and with another back-up if things go pear-shaped, they seem to have been able to revise and study more. Our head of Year 11 talked to some of those who fell into this category and they confirmed what Relate were telling us. They really could work better since having sessions with the counsellor. One clear example was this lad whose parents split up some months ago. He's been very angry at his dad, blaming him for it all apparently and acting out at school. The counsellor seems to have given him the chance to come to terms with all that. He's a bright lad, and with some of the pressure and anger eased, he got on with his revision. As a result he got five A's, and five other passes at B and C. A few more changes like that will certainly make a difference in an OFSTED inspection!

But it's not all about that. I really am interested in the welfare of all our students. I think we care more than we did in my days at a grammar school in Barnsley. I wouldn't want to go back to those days. We've got a good staff here who do a lot for our children, but Relate have supported what they do. We wouldn't want to be without their counselling now.

DATE NIGHT

Part 3

Lisa could still feel the catch in her voice when she breathed in. She knew Jay was aware of it. Something inside him seemed to have changed. It was hard to understand, but it felt like some kind of layer had been stripped away. She watched him as he walked back to her from the bar holding their drinks in his hands and for the first time in ages beneath the tears, the old excitement whenever she saw him stirred within her. She smiled as he put her fruit juice in front of her and sat down next to her with his pint.

"I'd better drive us home," she said.
He grinned. There was no resistance. And then, unexpectedly, there were tears. Not the tiny leak from the counselling room, but tears flowing down his cheeks. She drew him towards her and held him closely. Suddenly, almost as if she could see it happening in front of her, it felt like the shell that had surrounded him for so long broke into pieces and in her arms once more she was holding the real Jay.

She was glad they'd chosen a corner spot away from anyone else's sight. She could feel her own tears flowing too, but not now from sadness. More, she could feel relief at what was happening. Gradually the intensity of his feelings seemed to subside. This is like holding Tom or Max she thought to herself. Men! Why do they do this? But maybe it was just this strange otherness in males that made her love them. Boys, men, inside they were all the same.

He was stirring again now.
"Lisa . . ." he said.
"It's alright Jay. We can work it out."
"Mmm. I want to. I really do."

"I know. This is the starting point."

He was sitting up now. His hand found hers.

"Drink up," she said.

Dutifully, as if he was one of the boys, he did as she said.

"She's good isn't she."

"Who is, Jay?"

"Natasha," he said gesturing across the road to the Relate office.

It took a moment to work out what he meant.

"Tanya, you mean."

"Is that her name?"

"The counsellor, yes."

Laughter was in his eyes now. He'd never been much good with names.

"So you'll come back next week?"

"Booked it haven't we?"

"Just checking," she said, smiling.

*

As Jay drove to work, Rachel was on his mind. She'd listened sympathetically when he'd told her about Lisa. 'I don't think she fancies me anymore,' he'd said.

"That's a shame. Everyone needs to be loved. We all do," she'd said.

There was something encouraging about the way she'd said it, like 'maybe I could do that for you'. Nothing much had happened after that. He hadn't really expected it to; not first time anyway. But the promise was there in the way she'd brushed against him a couple of times, and the very friendly hug she'd given him when he left. Testing it out had definitely been on his mind. 'Why don't we do this again?' she'd said.

Now, after that counselling session, it felt different. Rachel suddenly felt like a threat; something he needed to extricate himself from before it was too late. Now he could still tell Lisa and that counselling woman, Natasha or Tanya, whatever her name was, that there was no affair. But he was sure now if he went to her flat again . . . 'Well, who knows?" he asked himself out loud as he stopped to let a mother and two little boys cross the road in front of him. All three of them waved at him as they crossed. He waved back and smiled. As he engaged the gear and drew away he could feel a wave of fear rising up his spine. They could be his family, and he was risking it.

Rachel was already in the office and bending over to the photocopier when he walked in. Her short skirt was revealing as she turned and looked up at him, smiling. He walked through to his own desk, aware that something had stirred in him again, and a few minutes later she was standing beside him.

"I'm working late again tonight," she said.

It felt like there was something else unspoken.

"I see," he said.

He could feel the excitement, but the fear feeling was inside him as well, mingling with it. He didn't know what to do.

"I could make you something to eat again, like last week."

He tried to say something but the words wouldn't come out.

"I don't know, Rachel," he said, "I really don't know."

*

Hope. That was what it was. Lisa could feel it just sitting tentatively inside her. She waved to Tom as he went into school, but as usual he didn't look round.

"Not bothered are they!"

Sian was standing beside her, waving at her own five year old who at least half turned and grinned before rushing off.

"No," she said. "Well, must get home now."

"Everything alright?"

"Yeah, cool," she said, surprised at the comment.

"Just you've looked a bit . . . well . . . down lately."

It felt like an invitation to talk. For a moment, temptation, but she held it back.

"The usual," she said, managing a smile.

"No, longer than that . . ."

It felt persistent. She didn't feel ready to talk, and maybe, with Tanya's help, she wouldn't need to.

"No really, I'm alright."

"Well . . . any time, you know . . ."

"Thanks," she said. Park the offer for a moment. Use it if she needed it later. She smiled again. Inside her it felt evasive, and it looked like Sian didn't really believe her. But it would have to serve for now. She turned and made her way home.

No she decided, quite firmly in her own head, this was hers to sort, hers and Jay's. Telling someone else felt like breaking a confidence. And it had seemed genuine when he told her there wasn't any affair. More than anything she wanted that to be true. And Tanya had reassured her they weren't alone. Many other couples had problems too. 'Keeps us in business' she'd said. Last night that hadn't seemed funny. Now she was aware of smiling at the idea. Perhaps Tanya really could help them to sort things.

More than anything, Jay seemed like he wanted it to work; something she'd been doubting. The relief of that felt like a great weight floating away from her. They were talking now, really talking. She was determined to keep it going.

*

The card from Mark and Jo cheered her. 'We're getting on famously now – like a second honeymoon! Thanks for everything xx'. Tanya smiled as she read it.

"Sometimes it really does work," she said.

"Often! Don't be pessimistic, we're often successful."

Margaret's round face above her bright red dress wrinkled as she grinned at her.

"Ever the optimist!" she said. "I sort of had Steve and myself in mind."

"Well you're just the counsellor! Seriously though, if you'd been to counselling, do you think you two might have stayed together?"

"Maybe. I've wondered that myself. But you can't go back. Life can only be lived forwards . . ."

"And understood backwards."

The round face was grinning again as it finished her sentence. She nodded.

"I'm hopeful about these two I'm working with now. She thought he was having an affair, that's why they're here. But he denies it."

"Don't they all?"

"Most of them. But I think he's telling the truth. Problem seems to be communication . . . or the lack of it. And sex of course."

"So what's new?" She ignored Margaret's cynicism. It was a front, not what she really believed, she was quite sure if that.

"I know," she said, "But every unhappy family is unhappy in its own way remember."

"Who said that then?"

"Tolstoy; Anna Karenina. You've read it no doubt?"

Margaret's face, a mixture of grudging respect masked in a grimace, made her laugh. It was always fun sparring with her.

She went through to the counselling room and checked through her notes. Lisa and Jay would be with her soon. Determined to succeed, she wanted to be ready. At the top of her notes was the reminder to herself, one of Margaret's favourite sayings: 'The desired outcome is what the clients want, not what you want.' Surely though, reviving their relationship was what these two wanted? Still, remembering that was her agenda was important. If Relate ran like her old school, she might well have had to write out Margaret's statement a hundred times.

*

"So, how has it been this week?"

Lisa looked at Jay sitting beside her. "Better," she said. The smile was faint, but it was there.

"Jay?"

He nodded, tried to say something and coughed instead.

"Sorry. Better, yes."

"Better?"

Reflect back what the client says; don't try to interpret too soon. It felt right. Tanya smiled, waiting for one of them to reply.

"We're talking again. It's like Jay's part of the family again."

"Jay?"

"Yeah. Feels better. Like she believes me now."

"Well you've been getting home earlier. . . ." Lisa said, looking directly at him.

Did he look guilty then; moving uncomfortably in his seat? Tanya wasn't sure.

"I've been making an effort," he said after a pause.

She nodded, waited for a moment, but it didn't seem like there was more.

"Talking is very important. But it can take time . . . when things haven't been too good," she said, ". . . building confidence again is important."

The body language in front of her was softer, but it felt somehow . . . fragile, like things could still slip. But she wasn't quite sure why she thought that.

"Last week you said something about a date night," she said, "I was wondering if you wanted to build one into your life again?"

Jay was nodding and Lisa was looking at him.

"O.K. by me," Lisa said, "but he's got to stick to it this time."

"Sounds like you don't quite trust him yet."

"No . . ." she said quickly, "I just need to be sure."

"It's not just me Lisa."

Jay's response came quickly, as if there was some agenda behind it.

"I want it to be like it used to be," he said.

"Can you say a bit more?"

"Well . . . more fun. Not always about the house and the children and things . . ."

Lisa's reply came quickly. "But that's what my life is at the moment. Don't you see that Jay?"

He turned towards her with his arms out as if to say, what can I do?

Continued on page 143

VOLUNTEERING

LIFE AFTER TEACHING

I had a great job as a primary school teacher, working with nine and ten year olds. I did it for nearly forty years. There was no break in service for me because I haven't had children. That's something I've regretted, but it just never happened for us. Eventually Brian and I were very philosophical about it. We just accepted it wasn't meant to be. He filled his life with his own work as a surveyor and I had all those other children's lives to develop.

Brian was two years older than me. He took retirement before me, and I retired when I got to sixty. We planned to spend more time on our garden and to do a bit of travelling. For the September after I finished, we booked a Mediterranean cruise. It was really enjoyable, and helped me to overcome the withdrawal symptoms from all those lovely children with their excited faces coming in to start the new school year.

We got back, and on the Sunday after, Brian suddenly didn't feel well after our lunch. He stood up to go outside to get a breath of fresh air and just collapsed. I'll never forget the sight of him standing, holding his hand to his chest and just rolling forward onto the ground. Immediately I bent down to him, calling his name, but he was unconscious. The ambulance came within fifteen minutes and rushed him off to hospital while I followed in the car.

They took him into emergency resuscitation. Already I'd come to the conclusion he'd had a heart attack. I just concentrated on what had to be done at first. My feelings were completely numb. Then everything changed when the doctor came out to see me. 'I'm afraid there was nothing we could do,' he said. I'm sure I said something silly like 'Thankyou'. When I went in to see him lying there my feelings were still disengaged. It was shock, I'm sure of that. I have no memory of driving home. I don't think anything really hit me until the day of the funeral. I broke down completely then.

The year that followed was the loneliest year of my life. My former school colleagues and friends were very kind. They came and talked with me and took me out whenever they could. But there was a deep well of loneliness inside that I knew would never really go. Life seemed repetitive and without meaning. Sometimes I walked the local high street aimlessly just wishing there was something I could do.

One day I walked past the Relate charity shop and read a notice in the window. 'Volunteers wanted' it said. Impulsively I went inside and talked to the manager. She was very interested in me. She told me her name was Bonnie, which seemed an appropriately friendly name and also told me a bit about the charity and what it did. The retail shops raised funding to support the counselling work. Apparently charity shops are always looking for volunteers. They help to get key things done without being a drain on scarce funding. There and then I decided it was what I wanted to do. And it only took a couple of week to do the checks that had to happen.

When I got home that day I suddenly wondered what I'd done. After all, I could be doing supply teaching work in schools. But I'd turned down invitations in the past and still didn't feel it was what I wanted to do. Too much like revisiting the past. I'd always thought when I retired that would be it. But working in a charity shop? That was something else as the youngsters say. But as a teenager I'd worked in shops to earn money for my studies. I didn't need to earn money now, but I did need company and a purpose in life. Along with the anxiety there was a real feeling of excitement. When I turned up for my first day I was nervous of course, but it felt really good.

Our shop has three volunteers. Between us we make sure the full time manager is never left on her own. On Saturdays, our busiest day, there are two of us as well as Bonnie. I'm amazed at how many people come into the shops. Most of them buy something. Some just come in to talk. That's alright as far as I'm concerned. Shops provide a social purpose in our society. It's not all about selling. One of the things I like to do is talk about what Relate actually does. I've learnt quite a bit over the year I've been volunteering and I talk as if I know all about it. I don't of course, but I do support everything the charity does.

Quite a lot of the work is backroom activity. I receive donations, sometimes delivered hastily in black sacks while a car is parked on a double yellow line outside. I sort through it and separate out what we can sell and what we can only dispose of. Even clothes we can't sell can still help us because we get paid by weight for it when disposing it. It's not much, but every little helps, as another rather more wealthy retail company puts it.

People bring in all sorts of things for us to sell and we're grateful for everything, even if it only raises five or ten pence for the charity. Quite a lot of stuff comes from house clearances when people have died. One man brought in nine umbrellas. He said they were his mother's and he laughed when he told us that. Apparently she was obsessed with not getting her hair wet and always made sure she had an umbrella in every bag or handbag!

We also have a van that travels around the area picking up goods that people offer us and moving things around between our charity shops as appropriate. When the van arrives at our shop, I help to unload or load it as appropriate. I like to think I'm still fit, although that's not a requirement. The other two volunteers in our shop are older than me and less able to lift things. That's not a problem. Age is no barrier, and I believe a volunteer in another shop is over eighty. Volunteering is worthwhile however old you are.

As well as meeting a lot of new people, and actually finding new friends, I've really found something that makes life meaningful for me. Time passes very quickly when I'm working. And there are amusing moments. One Saturday afternoon two boys of about twelve or thirteen were messing around outside and making a nuisance of themselves. They wouldn't move when the shop manager asked them to. I went out to see if I could help, and as soon as they saw me they ran off. They were boys I'd taught in my last year before retirement! Teachers sometimes have that effect.

I haven't regretted being a Relate volunteer. It's a complete change from being a schoolteacher; a totally new career. But it really is fun. I hope to be able to go on doing it for quite a while. Sometimes I wonder what Brian would have thought of me doing it. Occasionally I imagine him looking down at me and laughing. I don't think it's what he would have done if I'd been the one who'd died. But you never know . . .

VOLUNTEER BETTY
MEETS BUFFY THE VAMPIRE SLAYER

It's not every day a member of the air ambulance crew wants to find a buffy the vampire slayer costume for a fancy dress party. But Jason did, and he'd heard that the Relate charity shop on Whitchurch Road outside Shrewsbury town centre had just what he wanted. Cathy the manager was very happy to find it for him. The shop had the full gear; shoulder pads, ribbed tights, a very short leopard skin skirt and a wig which would cover his shaven bald head. Jason was allowed into the small staff area behind the shop, where he could try everything on. The two female volunteers couldn't resist a peep as Jason dolled himself up and there was a lot of laughter coming out of the back office, before he was ready for his grand entrance out into the shop front.

And Jason's timing could not have been more immaculate. At the very moment he made his appearance, another volunteer member of the shop staff made her entrance through the front door, reporting for duty. No ordinary member of staff either. Betty Gittins was ninety, fit and energetic as anyone twenty five years younger and Relate's oldest volunteer. Cathy was standing next to Jason when Betty came through the door. She recalls the astonished look as she came in that afternoon.

"There was a moment of absolute disbelief on her face," she says, "like, what on earth am I seeing? She didn't swear of course, women of her generation mostly didn't, but her eyes widened and her mouth opened as if she might be going to say 'bloody hell', or something like that. But she's quick to catch on is our Betty. The shock very quickly turned to a delighted grin as she realised she was looking at a man in drag. Her eyes sparkled and I could see other words forming in her head. 'Don't you think that skirt's a bit short, dear?' was what she said."

It's just as well there were no customers in the shop at that moment as everyone collapsed into uncontrollable laughter. They would probably have shot out again thinking they'd entered a mad house. The story is one told over and over by those present, and retold by all those who have heard the story since.

Betty's story

Betty's daughter Jane provides the background to
a very special life.

Relate volunteer Betty Gittins the youngest of three daughters, was born in 1916 to John and Lucille Parton. With husband Leslie she had three children and four grandchildren, and was passionate about all creatures great and small. She never said no to any animal needing a home, and at one time had 3 dogs, 11 cats and Peter the Green Amazon parrot! She was always busy. Apart from children and animals, she loved crosswords, and read a great deal, often finishing a book in a day. As if all that wasn't enough, she flew on Concorde and cruised on the QE2.

She even met the Beatles! Just before they were famous her daughter Gloria went to see them at the Music Hall and waited for them to come out from the back door. After they gave her their autographs they asked if there was anywhere they could get something to eat. Gloria said that she didn't live very far away and that she was sure her mum would make them a sandwich and they could have a drink. When she got home Betty asked her if she had seen 'those Beatles'. 'I've brought them with me,' Gloria said. They had sandwiches and a drink before leaving to go back to Liverpool.

But then Betty's life changed. Leslie died suddenly when she was just 65, and ten years later Gloria died as a result of a car accident. She was devastated. For months, life seemed to lose sense and purpose. Good friends did what they could to help, but an important turning point came when her friend Lin Foley, at that time Chief Executive of Relate, asked if she would like to volunteer for the charity. At first unsure, Betty went along to the Relate Charity Shop in Claremont Street, Shrewsbury to do 'just a few hours a week.' But she soon grew to love the contact with staff, other volunteers and the people who came into the shop to explore and buy. Those 'few hours' soon became a few days working for a charity whose aims she supported wholeheartedly.

And when Relate opened another charity shop in Oswestry, although Betty was over 80, she was asked to spend some time helping to establish that shop. Distance was no problem! Locals got used to seeing her boarding the bus to her new challenge. She embodied the Dunkirk spirit, travelling wherever she was needed in all weathers, sometimes less than fully well. Despite another tragic loss in her life when one of her grandsons died as a result of a holiday accident, Betty continued volunteering for Relate through to 2007. Then aged 91 and Relate's oldest serving volunteer, she finally had to retire due to failing health.

A unique and very special person, Betty touched many lives. She was a generous spirit, loved and respected. Her family and all the people she met through volunteering were her life. Since her death in July 2009 at the age of 93 she has been much missed. But her memory lives on in the hearts of all of those who knew her.

RESCUING THE WEDDING GUEST

The young man who came into our Relate charity shop that morning looked lost. He was tall, mid-twentyish, with that dark unshaved look the youngsters have these days. My daughter says it's called designer stubble. I asked if I could help him.

"I'm going to a wedding in an hour," he said.

In an old tee shirt and a scruffy pair of jeans, he certainly didn't look like that was where he was going.

"The trouble is, I've forgotten to pack a shirt."

"I see," I said, beginning to catch on.

"And I need one now."

I knew we had some shirts on our racks so I got his collar size and began looking through. It wasn't long before I found one that seemed just right. I held it up for him to see. No doubt it was a good shirt, clean, but a bit crumpled. The label on it said £4. Quite a bargain I thought as I told him the price.

He looked at it, nodded, then seemed to want to say something else. I waited.

"You couldn't . . . iron it for me could you?"

He had that half-guilty, half flirty smile on his face as he said it. I couldn't help grinning back. He was a good-looking young fella after all.

"I could steam it for you," I said.

"Would you?"

His face was suddenly animated and the smile really widened.

"Just give me a few moments," I said, taking it through to the back room.

It didn't take me long to freshen it up and remove the creases. When I went back into the shop he was looking anxiously at his watch. Seeing me, he looked up expectantly, and when he saw the shirt, smart and ready for wearing, the big smile was back.

"Thankyou, I'm really grateful," he said.

"You have got a tie, have you?" I said.

"Oh yes, I remembered that."

"you'd have looked funny with a tie and no shirt."

From his back pocket, he took a five pound note and handed it across to me.

"That's fine, I don't want any change."

He didn't want it in a bag; just took it out of the shop on the hangar. He'd told me his hotel was almost next door. That's one satisfied customer I thought, and a bit more to keep the charity afloat.

Twenty minutes later he was back in the doorway. And what a transformation, there was! He had a smart light grey suit, polished black shoes, a blue tie with some kind of badge on it, and of course, the shirt.

"Well don't you look the part now," I said, "it's not you getting married is it?"

"Best mate," he said, "I'm still looking."

It made sense, I guessed a girlfriend would have made sure he remembered his shirt. But I didn't think he would have to wait too long. If I'd been forty years younger . . .

Then, thanking me again, he was off to the wedding.

I carried on with my job, sorting clothes, serving customers, all in a day's work for a Relate charity shop volunteer. Then I heard the bells from the church up the road, and I imagined my young man with his charity shop shirt. I wondered if he was telling his mates about what happened. Somehow I guessed he would, over a pint or three later. He looked like he could enjoy himself.

DATE NIGHT

Part 4

"What are we talking about here?"

Jay knew the answer immediately, but how could he explain? Lisa came to the rescue.

"It's sex. He says I'm always too tired."

"Well that's what you always say!" He could feel himself getting angry. "That's what date night was supposed to be about."

"No Jay, not just sex. It was about us finding time for each other. You didn't give it a chance."

He wanted to deny it, but somewhere inside him he sensed there was some truth in what she was saying. Tanya was looking at him as if she expected his version. Once more he felt outnumbered. There were two women and just him. He had to fight his corner.

"Men have . . . different needs," he said eventually.

He could see Lisa wanted to answer but for once Tanya cut in.

"Maybe we just have to understand each other's needs better?"

Lisa was nodding, agreeing.

"If we don't try to understand each other, a lot can go wrong in a relationship."

He wondered once more whether to say anything about Rachel, but it felt dangerous. After all, nothing much had happened. He'd sorted it just in time.

"That's when suspicions can creep in," Tanya was saying.

"Like when I thought Jay was having an affair?"

Were they reading his mind?

"I haven't Lisa, honest."

"You swear to me?"

Impulsively he changed his mind. "There was this girl, in the office. She tried to chat me up."

They were both looking at him. He couldn't stop now.

"If I'm honest, I was tempted. But I swear to you, nothing happened."

For a moment there was silence. Lisa looked at him as if she was judging him, like weighing up what he'd said. Then, to his surprise she put her hand across and took his.

"I'm glad you've told me."

"I wanted to tell you," he said. It felt like a lie at first, but as he held her hand he knew suddenly that he had wanted to be honest really. It was fear that had held him back.

*

"Go alright?"

Margaret stood filling the doorway, looking surprisingly like a large wasp in her yellow and black striped dress. Tanya couldn't help thinking her skill as a supervisor was in inverse proportion to her dress sense. She could discuss cases and get a second opinion without breaking confidentiality.

"Think so. The guy says he didn't have an affair. Some sort of flirtation, nothing more it seems."

"Do you believe him?"

"She does. Looks like she wants to."

"You?"

The searching eyes were on her again.

"He seems genuine. Familiar problem of sex dropping off after the children, and him struggling with that."

"How can you check it out?"

Tanya thought for a moment. It wasn't a question she'd asked herself.

"Her reaction I think. I'm sure she'll have quizzed him when they got home."

"You'll explore that next week?"

"Mmm"

Afterwards she thought about it again. Something about Jay said he was telling the truth. She was almost sure of it. It hadn't been like that with Steve. Looking back on it, she could see she'd never really trusted him. Wanted to, certainly, persuaded herself for a long time everything would come good. Even when Louise and Chloe were small and he came home late with some plausible excuse she'd chosen to believe him. Youthful rose tinted spectacles? Perhaps; but who wants to believe their partner might be having a secret affair? Now she knew her default position was very different. It was one reason why she was inclined to trust her instincts with Jay and believe him. It *wasn't* how she'd normally expect herself to respond. But Margaret was right. Understand what's going on inside you and then check it out carefully. Heart first, then head. Check it out next week.

*

Tom was fractious; struggling to settle down to sleep.
"I think he might have a bit of a temperature," Lisa said.
"Have we got a thermometer?"
"Over there Jay. In that cupboard."
She watched him as he searched, then found it.
"I'll go and check," he said, "shall I take some Calpol up too?"
"Would you?"
"Of course."

Was he trying harder? It certainly felt like it. She finished putting the tea things in the dishwasher and started it.
"Only slightly," Jay said, coming back into the kitchen. "I've given him a spoonful to settle him."
She walked through to the living room and sat down. The screen told her CBeebies was finished for the evening so she turned the television off as Jay walked through. Then once he'd settled beside her, she turned towards him.
"Jay."
"Mmm?"
"You know what you said last night?"
"What did I say last night?"
"With Tanya. About that girl."

"Oh. Yeah."

"It was the truth wasn't it?"

"Like I said, she tried to chat me up. And because things . . . like, things weren't working out for us, I went along with it for a while."

Suddenly she was anxious again.

"Went along with what Jay?"

"Talking, laughing a bit, nothing more."

"You are telling me the truth aren't you?"

Something about his face said he was. She wondered whether to turn the TV on, but he was turning towards her.

"Lisa, I really do want this to work for us."

He was looking directly into her eyes, and she stared back at him. She could feel a kind of excitement moving inside her, like she'd always used to feel.

"Thanks for sorting out Tom," she said, but the words came out softly, like a peculiar chat up line. He moved closer, putting his arms around her and she responded. Soon his lips were on hers. After a while he lifted his head and spoke.

"Shall we go upstairs?" he said.

"Why not? It is date night."

He nodded, grinning, and quietly, almost secretly, like intruders in the night, they both stood up from the sofa without breaking contact and made their way out of the lounge.

SUPERVISION

Getting the quality control right

Liz Todd, senior supervisor for Relate Shropshire, Herefordshire and North Staffordshire, answers some questions

How do you know your counsellors are doing a good job?

It's really important to Relate to ensure high quality counselling. Our answer to this is proper oversight of what our charity delivers from week to week. For an hour and a half every month each of our counsellors has to have a one and a half session with me or one of my two colleagues. We call this supervision.

What do they have to do in their supervision time?

In confidence, without using the proper names of clients, they must review their practice over the month. This means identifying those cases where they have particular worries and talking about how they plan to proceed with the clients. This lets me know if they are making good enough progress. Where problems are identified, we can talk through ways forward.

What happens if you think a counsellor is getting something wrong?

We have counsellors trained to very high levels. Relate is accredited by the *British Association of Counselling and Psychotherapy* and our counsellors must follow their clear guidelines. But nobody is perfect.

My job in supervision is to ensure nothing important is missed, and to explore with the counsellor whether in any of their current cases their own issues might be getting in the way.

What do you mean by 'their own issues'?

Counselling is a very demanding role. It requires the counsellor to use not just their training but their own personal experience of life to help clients move forward with the problems they identify. Counsellors have to do this without talking about themselves. The time in the counselling room is exclusively for the clients. But because we're all human and because counsellors mustn't talk about themselves, there can sometimes be a hidden agenda.

Can you explain that?

Can I start by pointing out the obvious? In almost all couples counselling there will be two women and one man, or two men and one woman. This creates a potential problem from the start and our counsellors have to be aware of it. Most of our counsellors are female, so I'll use that as an example. What the couple come into the room with, we call the 'presenting issue'. Suppose that issue is a brief affair that the man has had. The couple say they want to get on with their lives and stay together. This is actually quite a common presenting problem. But suppose, a year before, the counsellor's husband has left her after an affair. In her own relationship it was an issue they couldn't resolve between them.

From here, two possible problems emerge. The counsellor can feel sympathetic to the wife and not see enough of the husband's perspective. Whatever our personal views by the way, we don't talk about 'wrong' and 'right', only issues to be resolved. Alternatively the counsellor might want to 'solve' a problem she couldn't solve in her own life. The counsellor has to empathise with both partners in the room as well as being objective in finding the way forward.

Empathising with the wife more than the husband is likely to lead to an unbalanced approach.

Can you really overcome that?

You can, yes. It's quite specific in training that counsellors learn to empathise with both genders. That also by the way applies to different sexual orientation, since Relate also works with gay couples. Our counsellors definitely can do that, as long as they recognise their own 'issues', which is our jargon word for personal problems. That's dealt with in our very rigorous training programmes, and counsellors have to keep up to date like everyone else, through CPD, which is another piece of jargon for Continuous Professional Development.

What if the counsellor doesn't tell you her own issues?

I'm glad you asked me that! We do ask our counsellors to disclose the issues in their personal lives which might affect their work. In supervision I would hopefully spot potential problems where a counsellor's issues could interfere and bring them to the surface in supervision. Since Sigmund Freud's work a century ago, we've known that the source of a lot of difficulties is the issues we don't understand about ourselves. Bring them up to the light and they can usually be resolved. That is after all what happens in the counselling process. We want to give clients the tools to help themselves.

But what if you don't spot the problems either?

That's possible of course. I've said nobody is perfect, and that includes me! But we do have another fail-safe. We have something called group supervision. This happens once a month. All counsellors in one area gather together with me, or one of our other two trained supervisors to discuss cases as a group. This is also confidential; no proper names emerge. One or more of our counsellors presents a case. Almost always this is a case where the counsellor feels they would value some input from their colleagues. The other counsellors comment on what they observe and suggest additional and sometimes alternative ways forward. Counsellors really welcome these sessions.

You expect a lot from your counsellors.

We do! It's a very demanding job. We limit the amount of hours any one counsellor does in the course of a week to twenty hours. The British Association of Counsellors and Psychotherapists advise this and we agree. Twenty sets of clients' problems at any one time is a lot to think about. Generally our counsellors do considerably less than that in a week.

Do counsellors actually enjoy what they do?

Most definitely they do. It's hugely challenging, but very rewarding too. A counsellor can change a person's life for the better; transform their existence in fact. That's a really big thing to be able to say and do.

WHY DO THEY DO IT?

Volunteers, counsellor's (and their partners) tell their personal stories

WHY I'M A RELATE COUNSELLOR

Like many people who decide to go to a counsellor, our marriage difficulties started after the birth of our first child. After seven years of marriage, the adjustment needed to cope with a very fractious baby proved too much for both of us. It didn't help that I was suffering from Post Natal Depression and I know I became very difficult to live with.

We did the obvious things – I visited my GP who said it was possible to get through this without pills. I was encouraged and grateful that she was so positive and with lots of support from friends and family, I began to feel more able to cope. My husband booked a break at a beautiful hotel, with a baby listening service, so that we were able to enjoy the lovely food in a calm atmosphere. Once back home we joined a baby-sitting group, so that we could start going out together again and kind friends supported us through broken nights and feeding problems etc.

On the surface we looked like the ideal family. Our son was thriving, we had our own house, my husband had a good job and we were surrounded by a loving supportive family and good friends. So what was the problem? Well a number of things really. I found the pressures of being a mum left little energy for anything else and I began to see the intimate side of our marriage as just another pressure. My husband, who'd struggled to support me and keep me calm during the post natal depression felt rejected and wondered where our happy marriage had gone.

We began to row as never before and became more and more short tempered with each other and the baby, as broken nights began to take their toll and the atmosphere grew tense. I felt guilty about everything and unable to talk to anyone about it, since I seemed to "have everything" whilst in reality my world was falling apart around me. In the end I realised nothing was going to change and I just had to talk to someone, so with my husband's agreement I made an appointment to see a Relate counsellor on my own, as I saw it very much as my problem.

I didn't get off to a very good start, as in the process of going into a multi-story car park, I managed to clip the front wing of the car. In a panic I quickly reversed only to catch the other wing on the way out. Eventually I found somewhere else to park and went in for my appointment.

I only have a hazy memory of that first session (over thirty years ago now) but two things really stand out in my mind. One is that for the first time in months, I was able to let everything out (tears and all) in front of someone safe. The other is that the counsellor somehow gave me permission to have these feelings of guilt, fear, anger etc. and accepted me without judgement.

The relief I experienced when I came out was amazing, together with a sense of hope that at last something could and would be done. By comparison the car damage seemed irrelevant and as always my husband was brilliant about it. He subsequently came with me for a course of counselling sessions, during which we gradually started talking about what was really bothering us and with the help and support of our counsellor and her very practical suggestions, began to repair our relationship.

I won't say it was an instant fix. We still had to face the many pressures that every couple with a new baby has to cope with, but we now had some tools to help, the main one being the ability to talk to one another sooner rather than later. We went on to have a second child with no recurrence of the post natal depression and found ourselves enjoying the process in a way we could never have imagined a few years before.

We got on with our lives, but the memory of that counsellor never left me (I can still remember her name). It was as if a small flame had been lit in me that day, in the middle of all the chaos I was experiencing. It was a flame that never went out and gradually grew into a passion for working with relationships. However, for years there was no opportunity to do anything about it, but when at last I was able to stop full-time work, I knew I wanted to train as a counsellor.

That was some years ago now and I've never ever regretted it. I shall always be grateful to that counsellor who gave me such hope when I was at my lowest ebb. To have the privilege of being able to do something to help others as I was helped, makes every session with clients very special. It keeps me just as motivated and excited with the potential for restoration today as when I first started training.

A DIFFERENT KIND OF CARE

I spent 15 years in teaching and a further 15 years working in the NHS in a variety of roles. A number of years ago now I became a Relate counsellor. It's a role I really enjoy, so when asked to contribute to this book about Relate, I was very happy to say why counselling is so important to me.

Relate training is very demanding. I already had counselling qualifications, but Relate training required attendance one weekend a month for three years, hours spent writing assignments and supervised practice. But at the end of the process I had an MA in Relationship Therapy. It felt like quite an achievement. My training included what is called systemic counselling, which essentially looks at the whole 'system' in which a person operates, and of course much of that is within the family. I also studied psychodynamic counselling which explores the clients' family of origin and early experiences and how this might have affected the present.

Much of my work in Relate is family counselling. With several family members in the room together that can be demanding, but it's very important too. If the family situation has deteriorated so far that no one can really listen to anyone else, or pay attention to what other members are trying to say, they need this kind of help. My main role is to help all the family to understand their own needs, to understand each other's needs, and where these clash, help everyone to find compromises which will work through time. One of the most important tasks in family counselling is to enable children and young people within the family to have their say.

I work with couples too. When there are two adults struggling with a relationship, there is a similar need to help each person understand the other and to work towards a way forward which meets both their needs.

The world we live in now, with social media, face to face communication within families can actually be diminished. Parents, both in couples and family counselling, often complain their sons and daughters are always on line with friends and have no time to be involved in family activities. This can lead to all kinds of problems and resentments which they need help with.

I get a lot of satisfaction from being able to help people to really communicate with and listen to each other. When people feel valued and respected by each other there is a way forward. That can take a lot of work. I need all the skills I've developed in my training, my counselling experience and of course through my professional background. Changes need reinforcing, and that takes time. There is also a cost involved which not everyone can afford. I'm glad Relate has a bursary for those who find finance difficult.

And for me, there is immense satisfaction in being able to help families and couples towards a better shared life. They feel valued, and so do I when I can achieve it.

THE RELATE COUNSELLOR'S WIFE

One day, shortly after his early retirement from a high stress job in education, my husband announced to me that it was his intention to train as a Relate counsellor.

It was a bit of a surprise to me and I wasn't sure how I felt about it at first. It seemed a good opportunity for him to do something very purposeful. But there were little niggles working in my brain which I struggled to understand. When he started his training, those niggles became a reality. What would this do to our relationship? Training to be a counsellor, in my eyes, meant that the greater his knowledge grew the most he would be able to spot flaws between us. I didn't like it. I didn't like the fact he would be discussing emotional things with other people. It made me feel very vulnerable. Personal counselling which would potentially open more emotional doors was also part of his training. How would this affect the way he saw me and my quirky ways?

There were plenty of fears. At the time I was working as a district nurse and came across many patients who were extremely poorly, and some were dying. The emotional support I was able to provide them with was limited, I think, by the lack of training I had in this area of care. However on the whole I think I was able to provide support pretty well. One day I had arrived very early in the morning at a patient's house. She had just died. I was very close to this patient having cared for her for several months and her death hadn't been imminent. The shock I felt was huge. Her family were distraught. I was the professional who had to be calm and supportive whereas I wanted to sit and sob. As I left the house I pulled into a layby to give myself some recovery time. The anger hit me then. Where was my husband? He was training to be a counsellor in Rugby. I had been doing the counselling, supporting the bereaved family without the luxury of training. I was out there at the cutting edge. It flashed through my mind that they were a precious silly lot spending far too much time naval gazing and being self-indulgent. Irrational maybe, but it was how I felt that morning.

After the endless training which included some counselling work in the evenings we settled into a slightly chaotic lifestyle. I worked by day and got home in time to see him disappear out of the door. He got home late, very tired. Sometimes he was stressed; other times he was happy that there had been a breakthrough or a successful case had ended. Not the best way to be, but as long as he was getting something positive out of the experience it was fine with me.

Once our lifestyle had changed to accommodate counselling we both seemed to settle into a different but more satisfying routine. Both of us learned to adjust to each other's needs. The biggest surprise to me was that we had survived the experience and, if anything, our relationship developed in a way that was more intimate. We knew even more about each other and remained very close. That was such a relief.

He got great personal satisfaction being able to help people. The money earned was not significant or important. The increased understanding of human emotions was a real bonus as he has always been keen to share his knowledge. I never heard a word about individual cases although the curious side of my nature would have loved to. Confidentiality is so very strict in Relate this just never happened.

He has now retired from the counselling job he loved. We're both retired people but each of us stays very active supporting all sorts of other things. It's just the way we are and we won't stop as long as we can be useful. We like a purpose and all the skills learnt by him and which it feels like I have somehow imbibed come in handy at times in other areas of life too.

Relate training and counselling has its positive side for us all.

Afterword 4

I can see she's looking at me as if trying to work something out. Twenty five maybe, smart in a black dress with sleek dark hair over her shoulders and dark eyes looking at me. Rachel Forster the name badge says. It's not familiar but the eyes strangely are.

"David," she says, reading from my name badge, "my counsellor!"

Her arms are suddenly around me as she stretches up, spontaneously hugging me. Then, as she steps back the intensity of the smile transforms itself into a thinner distressed face looking across at me in a tiny room by the school library.

"Burns," she's saying, "I was Rachel Burns then."

The faces in my head merge, and I'm aware now of how the earlier face still exists within the later confident version glowing excitedly in front of me. How many sessions was it? Twenty maybe?

"I'm here because of you," she's saying.

Suicide attempt. Overdose when she was fourteen. Nearly died, and she'd really wanted to. School referred her. I let her talk, let her sit in silence with the murmur of other students beyond the counselling room door a constant presence. Helped her find meaning out of an alien existence.

Ahead of us now the speaker opening the conference is preparing himself. The power point presentation glows into life behind him. 'Working with suicidal thoughts' it says. We both look up at it.

"Thankyou," Rachel mouths at me.

She turns sideways to take her seat and as the houselights dim I notice she's pregnant.

THE AUTHOR

Alan Cooper is chair of trustees for Relate Shropshire, Herefordshire and North Staffordshire. Since retirement from his career in secondary education, Alan has worked as a Relate counsellor and served on school governing bodies. He also writes a weekly column for the Stoke Sentinel, answering questions about relationship issues.

Alan is a supporter of both Relate and Kidney Research UK. With his wife Jan, a kidney dialysis patient and trustee for Kidney Research UK, he has edited the book Staying Alive, which contains stories of dialysis patients and kidney transplant givers and receivers. It is available via the website http://www.thestayingalivebook.co.uk All proceeds from the book go to Kidney Research UK.

As Al James, Alan has also written eight novels. His website is http://www.aljamesauthor.com

He can be followed on twitter @aljames299